10,000

YEARS IN THE

SUBURBS

10,000 YEARS IN THE SUBURBS

BY

JACK ZIMMERMAN

FOREWORD BY ERIC ZORN

LAKE VIEW PRESS

For Mary Frances, who laughed every day of her life.

Copyright 1994 by Jack Zimmerman/Press Publications,Inc. All rights
reserved.
These columns are reprinted with permission from Press Publications
Newspapers.
Published in 1994.
Printed in the United States of America.

Library of Congress Cataloging-inPublication Data
Zimmerman, Jack, 1945–
            10,000 Years in the suburbs / [Jack Zimmerman].

            Author's columns originally published in Press Publications
            Newspapers
            ISBN 0-941702-38-3
            ISBN 0-941702-36-7 (pbk.)
            1. Elmhurst Region (Ill.)—Social life and customs. 2. Chicago
            Region (Ill.)—Social life and customs. 3. Suburbs—Illinois
            Chicago. I. Title. II. Title: Ten thousand years in the suburbs.
            F549.E42Z56   1994
            977.3'11—dc20   93-38852
                                                            CIP

Chapter 7: At the movies

Chapter 8: Music, Music, Music

Chapter 9: Huh?

Foreword

FOR NINE VERY LONG YEARS it has been my habit to read more than fifty community newspapers every week in search of little stories, goofy controversies and eccentric denizens of suburban Chicago. Every so often my hours of browsing pay off and I find something I can turn into a column in the Tribune, but the search is generally a mind-numbing labor that fills my head with news of tree-plantings, revised parking regulations and redirection of sewerage (which is not the same thing as sewage, something I didn't know before).

Jack Zimmerman's column surprised me when I first happened upon it tucked away in the middle of the Elmhurst Press. There, among the water commission stories, the endless letters to the editor about zoning and the features on people with large collections of bells or somesuch, was a caustic, literate voice commenting on everything from world affairs to the misadventures of his family.

I was hooked. From then on, when I would read my huge stacks of papers I spaced out the Elmhurst Presses, one every thirty or so, as a reward and a goal. Jack was about the most versatile columnist I'd ever read—sometimes he was bitter, sometimes he was deeply sentimental and sometimes he was hilariously funny. He was proud, he was self-effacing. He was angry, he was sappy. He was anti-suburban, yet quintessentially suburban—a writer fully in touch with the contradictions that dwell in all of us. Poor man.

So I sat down in the summer of 1987 and wrote Jack a fan letter, all the while thinking, *Wait a minute, I'm the guy at the big paper. He's the guy at the little paper. Shouldn't he be writing me the fan letter?*

But I mailed it off, and pretty soon he got in touch. We agreed to meet for dinner—with our wives along, in case the conversation got slow—at a Mexican restaurant in Bensenville. He was every bit as analytical, funny, neurotic and charming as his columns suggested, though slightly shorter, I should tell you.

Jack has done it all—been a Navy man, a starving musician, a piano tuner, an aspiring novelist, a magazine editor and a member of the nervous unemployed. He brings this experience as well as an uncommon insight to his prose, which I understand he composes in the middle of the night on a trashy little portable computer. To read Jack's columns is to get to know a remarkable man and an unusual talent.

Now forewarned, you readers of this book will be denied the pleasure of surprise discovery I experienced when chancing upon "Loose Change" in the Elmhurst Press. On the other hand, you can get to know Jack Zimmerman without having to eat suburban Mexican food. I think I'm still burping it up.

Eric Zorn

10,000 YEARS IN THE SUBURBS

10,000 Years in the Suburbs

10,000 Years in the Suburbs

EARLY ON WE HAD ONE KID and rented a house from my father-in-law. Ours was a working-class Chicago neighborhood where older people spoke Polish and younger ones dropped out of high school to learn body and fender work.

Neither I nor my wife had jobs. To scrape by we gave private music lessons in suburban high schools, and for a time I played trombone on WGN's "Bozo's Circus"—this after a lifetime of studying with Chicago Symphony players. Realizing I'd never make it in music, I spent a year in piano tuning school.

Later I came into some money; not a lot but enough for the down payment on a house. I wanted to buy the one we already lived in, but my wife would have none of it. "We should move to the suburbs," she said daily. "They have good schools and trees."

She was right. Our block had only one tree, and our son would attend a neighborhood school that was out of a Dickens novel. I didn't want to see the kid surrender to a lifetime of slapping Bondo on rocker panels when he turned 16.

I had grown up on the South Side of Chicago in a family that considered State and Madison Streets the center of the universe. Whenever relatives or friends told my family of their upcoming move to suburbia, my German grandmother gave them the exit interview. "What hundred west is that Wheaton place where you're movin'?" she asked.

When the future suburbanites informed her that the City of
Wheaton did not abide by the Chicago street numbering system, my
grandmother pressed further. "They have alleys out there?" After
that was answered with a negative, she concluded the interview
with, "I don't know why anybody would ever live in such a place."

My wife, though, had come from a family of non-ethnic suburbanites—people who didn't know that a shot and a beer was a single unit. Thus, we scoured suburbia for a house, finally buying one
in Elmhurst, 18 miles due west of State and Madison. My grandmother had passed on, but my grandfather kept up the family tradition. "How much ya pay for it?" he asked over the phone.

"Forty-nine, five."

"Brick or frame?"

"Aluminum siding," I said.

"You're spending that kind of money to live in a toaster?" My
grandfather was a former tool-and-die maker who had little respect
for anyone who used adjustable wrenches or who lived in less than
a brick house with tile roof and copper gutters.

Soon after moving I gave up playing the trombone and concen-
trated on building the Zimmerman piano empire. My days were
spent tuning pianos for suburban housewives, all of whom had a
story to tell. Eventually I bought a storefront where I rebuilt pianos
and became clinically depressed.

Halfway through my 10 years in business I joined the Lions
Club. Middle-aged men do such things. Only a few days after I
joined, the club's president proposed that I accept an office in
Liondom.

"You want to be Lion Tail-Twister or Lion Bulletin Editor?" he
asked. The choice wasn't difficult. Tail-Twister went to weekly
meetings and fined fellow Lions 25 cents for not wearing an official
Lions lapel pin. The Bulletin editor went to weekly meetings,
recorded all of the club's comings and goings and published them
in a weekly newsletter.

"Make me Tail-Twister," I said. He did, but withdrew the
appointment after discovering someone else had already accepted.

"All that's left is Bulletin Editor," he said. I took it but had reservations since I couldn't type and had flunked high school English

more than once.

In 1983 I wrote four humor columns and submitted them to the Elmhurst Press. After hearing nothing for months, I figured that my life would be spent repairing bad pianos and drinking bad coffee with suburban housewives.

In March of 1984 the paper's editor-in-chief asked me if I could regularly write something funny or at least interesting.

"Yeah," I told him.

"Good," he said. "You have a regular column. Any ideas for a name for it?"

"Final Notice," I said as my eye caught a Commonwealth Edison bill on top of my desk.

"Sounds too much like death," he said.

"How about Non-Sufficient Funds?" I said as my eye moved further across the desktop.

"Call it 'Loose Change,'" he said.

In the beginning I idolized S. J. Perelman, a humorist who worked for the New Yorker in the 1930s and '40s. "You write just like S. J. Perelman," a retired English teacher told me as I worked on her Steinway.

"Thank you," I said. "That's the best compliment you could give me."

"You're an ass," she said. "Go to the library and see the last time anybody checked out S. J. Perelman."

She was right. The last withdrawal of an S. J. Perelman book was in 1954.

I left the piano business eventually and edited a magazine. There I worked for a man who refused to use ZIP Codes and who regularly played with a remote-controlled submarine in the company swimming pool. My column recorded these things as well as my coping with a wife and two growing sons.

Through the years I paid attention to the daily and weekly changes in my life but was unaware of a more gradual transformation. It wasn't until my oldest left for college that it hit me—I had become a suburbanite. The banker who interviewed me for a home equity line of credit asked the obligatory, "Years at present address?"

"Ten-thousand," I replied.

■

Mr. Mom Saga Part 1

M Y WIFE LEFT TOWN ON business. Lucky for her I'm unemployed. Otherwise she'd have to worry about the kids being home alone, a dog with a bladder infection and the possibility of a daytime burglary or a missed water delivery.

"Your father would never do that," my mother said when I told her I was house-husbanding for five days. But my father would never do anything except paint an occasional room or tuck me in bed at night while explaining how a diesel works.

My mother's next question was expected. "What are you doing for meals?"

"We usually don't eat meals," I explained. "We graze." My mother's child-bearing years occurred during a time when kids walked to and from school, fathers arrived home from work every night at 5:45 and families ate together. She never experienced the joy of shuttling two mouth-breathers to soccer and baseball practices at opposite ends of the earth. Nor did her only son ever utter those horrible words: "Mom, I made the traveling team!"

It wouldn't have mattered, though. Whenever I asked her for a ride, her standard reply—the standard reply of all women of her generation—was the same: "Your father has the car."

And in my house, the father still has the car. I picked up my youngest from junior high on Friday.

"Can I ask some kids to sleep over tonight?"

"No," I told him. "Your mother is gone, and I think I have a malignant tumor pressing against one of my frontal lobes. No sleepovers."

"Hope it's not serious," he said.

By phoning only friends with the Illinois Bell Call Waiting/ Conference Calling option after arriving at home, the kid established a phone tree that included the entire male population of his junior high school.

The concept is simple. My kid calls Little Teddy. Once Little

Teddy is on line, my kid puts him on hold and dials big Ned. Through a series of top-secret manipulations, which I've never understood, my kid, Little Teddy and Big Ned can all talk to one another!

But wait. While Little Teddy is on hold he doesn't just see how many gummy Bears he can stick to the roof of his mouth. He uses his Illinois Bell Conference Calling option to dial up Dirty Al, who in turn calls a few others.

By 4 p.m. my kid announced that one of the kids from Suburban Call Net was having a sleepover and asked if he could attend. "No." I said. "You always sleep for two days after you go to one of those things."

Besides, it's customary for the sleepoveree to reciprocate, and I can't stand the kid who would be spending 12 hours under our roof. "What's that smell?" and "Don't you have a clean glass?" are two of his favorite questions.

My oldest kid was finally home from high school baseball practice, so I ordered an 18-inch cheese pizza and a six-pack of Coke. The pizza lasted as a complete entity for five-tenths of a second after its arrival. By the 1:20 mark, it was gone. The six-pack of Coke made it to 9 p.m. when I mixed a couple of rum and Cokes before attempting to iron a pair of my oldest son's octagonally seamed pants. "Where the hell am I supposed to put the crease?" I asked him, but he didn't answer.

I tucked in my youngest around 11:30. "Listen, kid," I said. "Did you know that diesels don't have spark plugs?"

Mr. Mom Saga Part 2

I MADE IT THROUGH THE FIRST day of single parenting without a mishap. But that was a school day, and parenting on a day the kids are gone doesn't require many brain cells.

Still, though, househusbanding without supervision can be dangerous. Only hours after my wife left, a woman from a chemical lawn service called and asked if a highly trained technician could take a no-obligation gander at my front yard.

"What do you expect to pay the bill with?" my wife would have asked had she been present, and another heated family argument would ensue when I proposed canceling our cable TV subscription to have a lawn we could be proud of.

Within an hour a guy in knee-high rubber boots and a reindeer sweater did a few laps around the house and left behind my lawn's report card:

"Lawn contains uncontrollable Nimblewill, Quackgrass and Coarse Fescue. Aeration recommended!"

I had to figure out a way to come up with 40 bucks a month while unemployed and without canceling cable, just to get rid of coarse fescue. And did aeration require us to evacuate the premises until the smoke cleared? I was scared and barely slept that night.

On Saturday morning my youngest son watched cartoons while eating Lucky Charms and milk from a Buick hubcap. "Turn off Elmer Fudd and clean up your room," I yelled at him while I was still in bed.

"I'm watching Paul Tsongas on CNN," he said, then left immediately on his Rollerblades.

The 17-year-old got up around 11, found another Buick hubcap and box of Lucky Charms and went at it. My wife was gone for two days and we had already consumed six bucks' worth of cereal. If these kids ate nimblewill, quackgrass and coarse fescue, my problems would have been solved. But such was not the case, so I bought six frozen pizzas and another box of Lucky Charms, figuring this should get us to Monday morning.

"What's for lunch?" the rollerblader asked around two. "You have a choice," I said. "You can either have tabouleh — a mixture of bulgur wheat, tomatoes, parsley, onion and mint — or a frozen pizza. Naturally, the kid opted for the frozen pizza, but had I offered him no choice, he'd have said, "Not frozen pizza again."

"That stuff looks like eyelids," my oldest son said of the tabouleh after finishing his daily 120-minute shower. He ate a frozen pizza too.

I pulled the same stunt for supper but substituted stir-fried tofu for tabouleh. On Sunday afternoon, rather than watch martial-arts movies with the sound turned off so we could make up our own dialogue, the two boys and I headed for the Oakbrook Center mall. We took my oldest son's car. Wow! You haven't lived until you've driven through the Oakbrook Center parking garage in a 1975 Chevy Monte Carlo that looks evil.

We'd sneak up behind a Mercedes or one of those dinky little $30,000 BMWs and watch the driver panic as he saw 4,000 pounds of rust headed for his trunk.

The most fun was getting on the tail of a Lexus or Acura, slipping the Monte Carlo into neutral and revving the engine until it backfired. But after a couple of hours and two tankfuls of gas, even that became tiresome.

We knocked off the last two frozen pizzas Sunday night. The next morning, the woman from the lawn service called at 7:30. "We won't be needing your service," I said. "Corporate transfer, we're moving to L.A."

It was a lie, but a small lie that saved us from canceling cable.

For want of profound kids and a lake home

I'VE ALWAYS WANTED TO write one of those lyrical change-of-seasons pieces that big-time columnists seem to hatch in the Sunday Tribune every fall.

They begin with the author, if male, closing up the lake house in Wisconsin while reflecting on the previous several summers. Such columns usually start with something like, "The sun was low in the sky as we slipped away from summer's sweet embrace, heading toward the city to hunker down for another winter."

I've never understood why so many writers begin "hunkering down for another winter" around the 15th of September, but they always do.

If the author of such a column is female, the result takes a more human approach, without the obligatory verb "to hunker" but with double the adjectives. "The large, orange sun was low in the azure sky as we slipped away from summer's sweet embrace. 'Mommy, I wish we'd never grow old, I want things to always be the way they were this summer,' my youngest related as a warm tear wended across my sunburned cheek. Indeed, the long, cold winter awaited us."

I've never written one of these columns because I don't have a summer home, and my mouth-breathers never say profound things the way female columnists' kids do. "The sun was low in the sky as we headed home from Builder's Square. 'You owe me twenty bucks for the pizzas I bought last week,' the kid said as a six-foot length of plastic pipe slid forward and struck the back of my head, causing me to hunker down in pain. Jeez, I thought, I gotta put up with stuff like this for another winter."

Of course, spring is another favorite of columnists. "The back of Old Man Winter finally broken, we headed north toward our Wisconsin lake house, not unlike wild geese returning to their summer digs."

Female columnists would add, "Annie sat next to me, her

body another year older. 'Do you think I'll ever have children?' she asked. 'When you meet the right man,' I said as I handed her her first training bra."

Without a summer home my seasonal column writing situation is hopeless. "Now that the back of Old Man Winter was finally broken, I took a good look at the yard. Damn, I thought. I wish I owned a smaller dog. And who the hell threw that training bra in the bushes?"

While spring may be the season of rebirth and the impetus for numerous columns on the coming six months of baseball, you can't beat fall for the feeling of a fresh start. Once you have children, your life is hopelessly in synch with the school year.

Every columnist worth his or her weight in predicate adjectives waxes nostalgically over the back-to-school experience. Those who suffered through parochial education are more gifted at this than their public school counterparts.

"Sister Mary Theresa gave me a stern look as we reviewed the first chapter of the Baltimore Catechism. 'It has only been two-and-a-half months since school got out for the summer, and you've already forgotten that God is a spirit who knows all things, can do all things and is infinitely perfect,' she said with a glower. I could only stare at my neatly pressed pants from Morris B. Sachs."

Naturally, those without the benefit of Catholic schooling have to draw on some other experience for their writing. "Mom sent me to my first day of junior high wearing a brand new training bra. It really itched, so I took it off and threw it in the bushes."

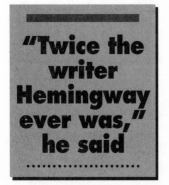

"Twice the writer Hemingway ever was," he said

M Y OLDEST SON NEEDED his Hemingway paper typed for his sophomore English class. "Can you do it for me?" he asked.

"Talk to your mother. I've got a column to write," I told him.

Unfortunately, his mother was busy gluing a mountain to the top of a shoe box for our youngest. It was one of those artsy projects his fourth-grade teacher dreamed up to assess our family's gene pool.

Our youngest, just back from a PTA book fair where he stung me for $13.62 for *My Teacher is an Alien* and *Funny Insults and Snappy Put-Downs,* busied himself balancing an egg on its end on a kitchen counter top.

This, he tells me, can be accomplished only on the first day of spring.

"Learn to type, will you?" I scowled at his older brother just like I do every time he hands me one of his papers.

Before starting, I lay down on the couch to catch a 20-minute snooze. Waking up with a start three hours later, I realized I still had to type through five pages of Hemingway machismo as well as knock out a column by the following morning.

"I'm going to bed," my wife announced. "I finally got the mountain to stick. Don't knock the egg over and see that the dog doesn't bite at his stitches."

Our springer spaniel had developed a fatty tumor on his back that made him look like the new Toyota Celica. We had it removed and the dog acted as if he missed it.

I started the Hemingway. Normally, I'm a modest person, but after just a few minutes I realized I'm twice the writer this guy ever was.

Consider that I knock off 104 columns a year, all of which are written at my kitchen table.

The TV is always on, my kids shake me down for lunch money and from time to time my wife interrupts my writing with little jewels like, "I want to live in a house that has architectural interest."

On the other hand, Hemingway would write a fish story every couple of years. In his spare time he hung around Paris with F. Scott Fitzgerald, sipping tall cool ones in the afternoon.

None of his kids ever asked him to take time out from *The Sun Also Rises* to type a term paper on Sherwood Anderson.

And look at his writing. "We made love. It was good." The guy won a Pulitzer for this stuff.

Of course, Dave Barry won a Pulitzer for catchy upper-case social commentary like "THESE PEOPLE HAVE THE INTELLI-GENCE OF POND SCUM," so I guess Pulitzers aren't that hard to come by.

I finished typing Hemingway around 2 a.m. and then worked a couple hours on this column, taking frequent breaks to pull the dog away from tugging at his bandage.

Sleep came easy at 4, and at 6:15 I returned to the kitchen table to finish the column. "Thanks for doing the Hemingway," the kid said as he headed for school at 7:20.

At 8 the egg fell over, and the dog finally ripped free of his bandage. The raised incision on his back made him look like a football instead of a Toyota.

My youngest busied himself with the egg on the counter top again, but he was now a day late.

"Will you forget about that stupid egg and get ready for school?" I yelled, struggling with the last few paragraphs of my column as "The Today Show's" Willard Scott did a weather report while being bench-pressed by a couple of bodybuilders.

My wife finally drove our youngest to school, and the dog, no longer fascinated by his recent surgery, slept in the sun by the patio door.

It was good.

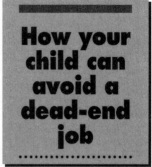

How your child can avoid a dead-end job

IN SEPTEMBER MY OLDEST STARTS his junior year of high school, a time when parents are supposed to take their kids and begin looking at colleges.

Unfortunately, higher education has become an expensive necessity in our society. Without it a person could work all his life at a dead-end job thinking that this is the natural order of things.

But give the same guy a four-year college education in which he learns to examine the nature of being and to question his existence, and he'll not only have a dead-end job for the rest of his life, he'll become clinically depressed, too.

Normally, choosing the right school would be really confusing, but lucky for me I've got *The Loose Change Guide to Colleges, Universities and Other Social Aberrations.*

Basically all forms of higher education fit into three categories:

• State Schools — places where students consume large amounts of beer and drive off-road vehicles.

• Hoity-toity private schools like the University of Chicago, where students read Proust for enjoyment and coeds don't shave their legs.

• Schools that advertise on cable TV, where students learn to drive 18-wheelers.

Of course, these fall into geographic sub-categories.

• Eastern schools — Strong liberal arts tradition. Students read *The Iliad* in Greek. Graduates usually go on to careers as arbitrageurs and eventually spend time in minimum security prisons.

• Midwestern schools — Emphasis on the technical fields, science and engineering. Graduates often become pitchmen for oil additives and 200-mile-per-gallon carburetors.

• California schools — Students go to them and co-habitate with members of the opposite sex named "Bunny" or "Todd." After graduating they work in health food stores and study tai-chi.

Living in the Chicago area, we are blessed with a number of

colleges offering enriching cultural experiences:

• American Islamic College, Chicago. Full-time faculty of one with six full-time male students and two full-time female students. Good points: 100 per cent of faculty has Ph.Ds! Bad points: limited social life.

• NAES College, Chicago. Started in 1974 for Native American Indians, the college has 24 full-time male students and 32 full-time females. Good points: SAT and ACT scores not required. Bad points: Classes meet during deer season.

• Spertus College of Judaica, Chicago. Established in 1925, offers undergraduate and graduate degree in Judaic studies. One full-time female student, no full-time males. Good points: Excellent faculty/student ratio. Bad Points: limited dating opportunities.

These are just a few bastions of higher learning in the Chicago area. Space does not permit me to list the more bizarre institutions such as the University of Illinois or Elmhurst College.

Just remember that while the cost of college is exorbitant, higher education is worth it. For the price of four new Audis, your kid will be transformed from an adolescent mouth breather to someone who can spot the difference between Gucci luggage and cheap imitations.

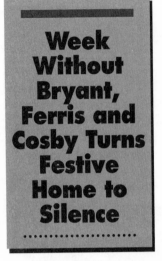

Week Without Bryant, Ferris and Cosby Turns Festive Home to Silence

SIGNED THE PTA, COLD TURKEY, one-week pledge of no TV, VCR, Nintendo and computer games.

"Why did you bring that stupid pledge home?" my oldest says to his brother.

"Do we have to do this?" my youngest asks. "Nobody else in my class is."

"Yeah, we have to do it. You'll thank me when it's over. And don't print your name on the bottom of the pledge sheet. Sign it and then let me see it," I scowl.

Monday. No morning "Today Show." How will Bryant ever get through the week without me? And I won't see Deborah wrinkle up her nose and look like Buffy on "Family Affair." You know Deborah's pregnant? The father's probably her husband. How does Willard dig up a fresh batch of 100-year-old geezers everyday?

Home from work at 6:45, wife gone. Ah silence! No "Hard Copy." Can eat a meal without teenage prostitutes, middle-aged Jell-O wrestlers or UFOs. Fix supper. Neither kid talks to me. "Can't we watch 'Fresh Prince of Bel Air?'" they finally ask.

"Ha, ha, sorry guys. A pledge is a pledge." They both stare at their food and don't say anything. Must be what it's like in the big house.

No Ferris Bueller! I hate that little twerp. Whatever happened to kids who respected their old man and wanted to be like him? Every time I see a teen-ager on TV, he's a wise-ass punk who needs his lights punched out. I feel better now.

Tuesday. Uh-oh, I forgot that this is Election Day. Going to be tough with no TV. Went to the polls. Anybody know what the trustees for the University of Illinois actually do?

Got to work late. "I cancelled your vote," I tell the boss. He doesn't laugh.

Did some food shopping. Got home by 7, quiet and the kids are doing their homework! God is in his heaven and all is right with the world. "What did you bring home for supper?" the youngest asks.

"TV dinners," I mock. The kid doesn't even smile.

It's 11 p.m. They're all asleep. I could turn it on for a few seconds and leave the sound real low. Catch a concession speech or two. Maybe Royko's on Channel 5 commenting on the elections. Speaking of Channel 5, is it Connie Chung or Linda Yu who wants to be with child?

Wait a minute, maybe Royko is on Channel 2 and he's punching Walter Jacobson in the face. Hate to miss stuff like that, but a pledge is a pledge. Can't let down now.

Wednesday. Morning was tough—election results just not the same on radio. Want to hear a depressing thought? Jesse Helms will be around another six years. Hello Philip Morris, goodbye National Endowment for the Arts.

Wonder what Deborah is wearing today, and does anybody know where Bryant buys his suits? Woman at work asks me how I'll live without "Twin Peaks" this week.

"Not watching it this year," I inform her. "Oh," she says and doesn't speak to me for the rest of the day.

No "Unsolved Mysteries" tonight. Probably Georgia rustics Homer and Belle get their pickup stolen by outer space aliens. Must be something about chicken-fried steak that does this to people.

Thursday. High point of the week. No Cosby! Justifies everything. Hate his kids. And those sweaters—c'mon.

But if I'm going to miss Cosby on Thursday, I'll also miss "The Flash"—average guy struck by lightening now wears Spandex and runs at 700 miles per hour.

Maybe somebody will tape it.

"Mind if I close your door? You keep moaning," he said

SOMEBODY ONCE SAID THAT being sick falls between being broke and being dead in the list of life's raw deals. I've been broke at times and after a recent bout with the flu, I recognize sickness as being worse than living without money. I can wait to see how being dead stacks up.

On Saturday morning it became evident that my youngest kid had the flu. He sat on the couch and stared at Saturday morning television in a zombie-like trance. But he always does that.

What tipped me off that something was wrong was when he said, "Dad, I feel terrible. I think I have the flu."

"Wait until your mother gets up," I told him. A kid isn't sick until his mother says he is. Besides, I don't like making executive decisions early on Saturday morning.

I suppose that if I were one of those organized parents I would have had everybody inoculated a month ago. But I've never taken the medical profession seriously; these are the people who once treated patients by opening their arteries to rid them of bad blood.

And what about all those stories of forty-year-old business executives who drop dead in hospital parking lots after taking stress tests? And wasn't Hannibal Lecter, the guy who liked to chew people's faces off, a doctor?

Anyway, by noon on Sunday it was apparent that I had succumbed. My body ached. I wanted to throw up, and I often felt dizzy. It was just like a hangover without the preceding pleasure.

When I got sick as a kid, my mother sat next to my bed and read James Thurber short stories to me. By the time I reached eighth grade I could recite "The Day the Dam Broke" from memory.

My mother made me a bowl of Campbell's tomato soup every

day for lunch and tossed a dollop of butter into it. It amused me to watch it dissolve.

Those days are long gone. Because I quit my job a month ago, my wife is now sole support of our family. "Don't get close," I told her. "You have another week of work before Christmas vacation."

It didn't do any good. She soon developed muscle aches and pains and an incessant cough.

My oldest son, who somehow avoided all this sickness, sat in the family room, only a few feet from my sickbed, and watched MTV.

"Mind if I close your door? You keep moaning," he said. It's embarrassing but true. I have a low threshold for pain of any type. But my moans were highly educational.

"Oh God, this must be what Solzhenitsyn suffered through in the gulag," was my most frequent.

My son wasn't impressed and continued watching videos that featured the rap group Public Enemy:

> *Never badder than bad 'cause the brother is madder than mad*
> *   at the fact that's corrupt as a senator*
> *Soul on a roll, but you treat it like soap on a rope 'cause the*
> *   beats in the lines are so dope*
> *Listen for lessons I'm saying inside music that the critics are*
> *   blasting me for*
> *They'll never care for the brothers and sisters and now across*
> *   the country has us up for war.*

"How am I supposed to recuperate listening to stuff like that?" I asked him. "Don't they have a rap video of something pleasant, like Joyce Kilmer's 'Trees?'" It was a stupid question and he didn't answer.

Solzhenitsyn hasn't suffered more than I have.

Even worse suffering — a Halloween sleepover

BY THE TIME YOU READ THIS, Halloween will have come and gone, and so will the sanity of thousands of parents.

Worried that an adult who spent his childhood deprived of parental love and a working Pez dispenser might pull the old razor-blade-in-the-apple trick or, worse, the old razor-blade-without-the-apple trick, moms and dads pace the floor waiting for their offspring to return from shaking down the neighbors.

For the following three days millions of hyperactive, sticky little grifters overdosed on sugar bounce off of any hard surface. It's tough to live with them.

Halloween has been with us forever, but so has the common cold, professional wrestling and politics.

Although it predates recorded history, the celebration of All Saints Eve in this country falls into four distinct periods.

1) Tired of sewing scarlet letters to everything that walks, early New Englanders have a costume party. "Look Martha! Miles is dressed as a Huguenot!"

2) During the Reconstruction, Rhett and Scarlett toss a little soiree. "Aunt Pity-Pat, why is Ashley wearing a carpetbag on his head?"

3) Exhausted from World War II, all parents from 1945 through 1960 make their kids wear Howdy Doody outfits.

4) Sometime in the late 1980s Elvira becomes the spokesperson for Coors Beer.

I've always liked Halloween. It's cheaper than Christmas and you don't have to watch football with your in-laws. But on the other hand, you don't get a day off, and nobody gives you soap on a rope.

My own experiences with Oct. 31 were mostly pleasant. Growing up I lived in a Lithuanian neighborhood where people handed out hard rolls with a piece of bacon in the center. I never got a sugar high but have had cholesterol problems since I was eight.

Although my childhood Halloweens were placid affairs, my adult ones were not. When my oldest son was 12 he hit me with a triple whammy: a sleepover on Halloween with his mother out of town.

I have suffered in my life, but with the exception of attending my draft physical and once reading the first chapter of Joyce's *Ulysses,* I have never suffered as much as I did that night.

Nine boys arrived in the early evening, then ate $24 worth of pizza while emptying a 55-gallon drum of Coke. Still fully charged from an afternoon of inhaling Sugar Babies, Dots and Gummy Bears, they worked off excess energy by playing jai alai in my living room fronton.

No sleepover is complete without the viewing of at least three movies that deal with mass murderers, serial killers or Okinawan kick-boxers.

Those we rented that night featured a lunatic behind a hockey mask who impaled rustics on spades, pitchforks and the hood ornament of a '53 DeSoto. Naturally, I watched all three videocassettes before guests arrived, just to make sure we were getting our money's worth.

And we were. Halfway through the second movie the body count had already climbed to 86 and that was without the benefit of automatic weapons.

By midnight I was exhausted, but the kids tapped a second 55-gallon drum and were still going strong. Retiring for the evening, I left them watching the guy in a goalie mask massage ingenues' bodies with a chainsaw.

I waited for a scary part, then jumped into the room wearing a goalie mask of my own. Those little, sweaty bodies will never forget that Halloween

I did it for parents everywhere.

Players change, but little boys' games remain the same

"BASEBALL CARD SHOW, Hillside Holiday Inn at 1," the kid instructed.

How are you getting there?

"No problemo. We'll get a ride from one of the other kids' fathers; we need you to pick us up at 2:30."

Two-thirty sharp. Just be ready.

"Did you collect cards when you were a kid?"

Yeah, but not the way you guys do. There were no card shows then, and if there were it wouldn't make any difference because my father wouldn't drive me anyway.

"So who did you trade with?"

I swapped cards with a fat kid with green teeth named Baby Joe. Eventually I tossed the cards and Baby Joe aside when I discovered Miles Davis.

"Who's Miles Davis?"

Jazz trumpet player.

"You know, if you had kept a 1951 Mickey Mantle card all these years, it would be worth $6,000."

Don't tell me stuff like that. I traded a 1951 Mickey Mantle card to Baby Joe. He probably still has it.

Any card you want me to get for you while I'm at the show?

Yeah, get anybody from the '59 White Sox.

"Like who?"

Start with Early Wynn and Billy Pierce. If you can't get them, try Fox, Aparicio, Jungle Jim Rivera or Sherman "The Tank" Lollar.

"What about Minoso?"

Forget Minoso; he played in Cleveland that year. If you really want to make my day, get Harry "Suitcase" Simpson's '59 card.

"What was he famous for?"

Not much. He had only a .187 average, but he hit a game-winning grand slam against the New York Yankees that summer. Sox fans remember him as the guy the team dumped to make room

for home-run slugger Ted "Big Klu" Kluzewski late in the '59 season.

"Where did Simpson play before coming to the Sox?"

Everywhere. Why do you think his middle name was
"Suitcase"?

"How much do you want to pay for him?"

Keep it under 10 bucks. But if you can't find him and Aparicio
and Fox are too expensive, there was another guy on that team I
was fond of. See if you can get me right fielder Al Smith.

"What was he famous for?"

He had a low batting average, and the fans always booed
when he'd strike out. To make him feel better Bill Veeck had an
Al Smith night. Anybody with a last name of Smith, Smythe or
anything close got into the ballpark for free.

"What happened?"

Smith dropped a fly ball, which led to a 7-6 victory for
Boston. I don't know why, but the guy always reminded me of
myself. In all fairness, though, he threw out Minoso at home plate
on an important play the night the Sox beat Cleveland to clinch
the Pennant.

"Was Veeck the guy with the exploding scoreboard?"

Yeah, he didn't have the scoreboard until the 1960 season, but
he did a lot of goofy things in '59. He tried to get Fidel Castro to
throw out the first pitch of opening day.

"You interested in any other cards?"

See if you can get me a Miles Davis.

Playing party boss to a pack of 11-year olds

I DISCOURAGED IT FROM THE start; nonetheless, my youngest had to have an eleventh birthday party.

Like most parents I harbor the gnawing fear that someday my kid will climb to the tower of the college he attends and begin blasting fellow students with a deer rifle. After his capture psychologists would disclose that because his father wouldn't let him have a birthday party when he turned eleven, he had developed these anti-social tendencies.

"He's inviting some girls," my wife cautioned me last week.

"Little young for that, isn't he?"

"They're just friends from school," she assured. She then explained that all this was to take place on an evening when she would be working.

The party was to start at 7 p.m. My wife leaves for work at 6 and I usually don't get home until 6:30. "Make sure he and his brother have the house clean," I instructed before leaving for work on the fateful day. Both kids sort of nodded, but that was all the commitment I could get from them.

I got home at 6:30. The kids hadn't done a bad job of cleaning the house. My sixteen-year old and three of his friends stared at the Nintendo mind control unit in the living room. "Why are these people in my house?" I asked with a scowl.

They didn't answer but continued working on Super Mario Brothers III. "This party starts in half an hour, beat it," I said to the sixteen-year old's friends. "And take your empty Coke cans with you." They made faces at one another and finally left.

"Put clean towels out in the bathrooms," I instructed the birthday boy. "And what am I supposed to feed everybody?"

"We're going to have pizza delivered," he said.

At 7 p.m. sharp all the girls arrived together. Giggling incessantly, they immediately sequestered themselves in the bathroom for several days.

At 7:02 the boys arrived and spent the next half-hour yelling stuff at the girls in the bathroom.

I took pizza orders. Almost everybody wanted cheese or sausage. One girl asked for spinach. "Shut up," I yelled at her through the bathroom door.

"Tell them that you're going to watch the movie," I said to the birthday boy, hoping this would dislodge the girls. They finally gave up on the bathroom and eventually watched the opening credits of *The Shining* with the boys in the family room.

Before Jack Nicholson and family ever made it to the Overlook Hotel, the kids bailed out of the family room and were back on familiar territory. This time the boys locked themselves in the bathroom and the girls giggled in the hallway.

"Hey, don't you guys want to see Jack Nicholson hit Scatman Cruthers in the chest with a fire axe?" I yelled to the seven boys in the bathroom. It did little good. They stayed in there until the pizzas arrived.

After eating four pizzas, which took 1 minute and 30 seconds, a few of the kids returned to the bathroom, but most stayed in the living room and listened to sanitized rap music.

The house was littered with cans of Coke that had one or two sips taken from them and like fine wines had been left to breathe.

At 10 the girls' parents picked them up. "Can some of the guys sleep over?" the birthday boy asked.

"Absolutely not, I hate children," I said. He laughed. The last child's parents showed up about five minutes after 10. "God, I thought they'd never get out of here," I said.

"How did it go?" my wife asked when she came home at 1:30. "Nobody's hurt and nobody died," I said.

Maybe an earring isn't so bad

MY FATHER WAS A MOST intolerant man in a family full of intolerant men. He felt that every American male regardless of age should have a military haircut, wear standard clothes (dark dress pants with a white shirt) and aside from a wrist-watch and wedding band, never wear jewelry.

Of course, this was for formal occasions. For everything else my father thought men should wear Oshkosh khaki work pants, flannel shirts and Knapp steel-toed work shoes. This included male children 6 and older.

"Look at the cut of that guy," he'd say when a neighbor kid would sport the latest D. A. haircut or wear pants that hung about his hips.

He once threw my uncle out of the house because he had shown up wearing an open-collared shirt and a gold chain. "The bastard looks like a gigolo, and on top of that, he didn't think enough of us to wear an undershirt," my father explained. "He's the kind of guy who should go into sales."

My German uncles, a gaggle of photo engravers, tool-and-die makers and Linotype operators, all nodded in agreement. Any man dumb enough to wear a gold chain under our roof deserved the bum's rush.

My errant uncle eventually did go into sales, confirming my family's long held suspicions about men who don't wear undershirts. At ensuing family gatherings he dressed conventionally, but everyone shied away from him because of his choice of occupation. "He's not even man enough to learn a trade," the others would say.

My father died in 1959. It was just as well; I don't think he would have survived the 1960s.

Saturday morning my 16-year-old son announced that he wanted to get his ear pierced. It wasn't a shock—he had sent up a trial balloon last April.

He was playing cards at a friend's house and had first launched the idea with his friend's parents. The next day the mother called and informed us of the aberration. "He's just saying that to see if he can get a reaction," my wife said. Such was not the case. He broached the subject several times in the following months.

Aside from my Germanic upbringing I could see no good reason for a sixteen-year-old kid not to wear an earring. My ancestors might have objected to this, but they were from a culture that produced the 300-day clock and the chicken dance.

Anyway, I gave the kid the keys to the car and he headed for Yorktown. About an hour later he returned. "They won't pierce your ear unless you are eighteen or accompanied by a parent," he informed me.

"Have your mother go with you," I told him. I had the time to do it, but aren't mothers supposed to handle stuff like this?

That night he played ball. "I see your kid's wearing an earring," one of the other fathers told me.

"Yeah," I said for the umpteenth time in the past couple of hours. "He's wearing an earring."

"I just hope he takes it off before his first job interview," he said.

"He's only a junior in high school. He's got a lot of years before he takes a job interview," I told him.

"He'll never work in sales," another father informed me.

"Every cloud has a silver lining," I said.

A bold move, but it's time to unplug the orangutans in Lycra

MY DEAR SON:
Sorry kid, but cable television is now history around here. I'm writing a letter this morning telling them to disconnect it. It was last week's "Music Video Awards" on MTV that pushed me over the rim.

I know this will seem like a radical step, but hey, this music video stuff is vile and disgusting. Seeing M.C. Hammer and company act like orangutans dressed in Lycra exercise shorts is hardly something I want in my home. Besides, dance numbers that center around pelvic thrusts make my neck hurt.

Continue your high school Latin studies. Coupled with the hours you've watched MTV, you're getting a good view of both the beginning and end of Western culture. I'll rent you some "Fred and Ginger" movies next weekend.
—Dad

Dear Cable Television Company:
Yes, I'm hopelessly addicted to CNN 24-hour-a-day news, and I occasionally view the offerings of one of your movie channels, although it is rare that I have the time when you have the movie. *Friday the 13th* and the *Police Academy* sequels hardly do it for me. Local community access channels are always good for a laugh, and the show with the bimbettes and the fast cars is as good as anything David Lynch ever did.

Nonetheless, it has come time for a parting of the ways. I've decided that with so much mediocrity in the world, I shouldn't have to subsidize any more of it. You see, television is no longer a reflection of our culture; it is our culture.

The other night when I watched a few minutes of the "Music Video Awards," I finally grasped the concept of "wilding." Thanks to technology, we have allowed our children daily visits from the cultural equivalent of professional wrestlers.

Of course, it's not your fault, you're just responding to the demands of the marketplace. Nonetheless, this has to stop. Unplug me.
—A Subscriber

Dear Arsenio Hall, M.C. Hammer and the Rest of the Cast of the "Music Video Awards":
I just thought you'd like to hear my latest rap:

You've got little talent and your art is shallow
What you do is of little value
Take away your speakers and your mixing boards
You've got the charm of the Vandal hordes

Hope you have many safe trips to the bank.
—A Former Cable Subscriber

My Dear Father:
Although you have been dead for some time now, your presence in my first thirteen years of life has forever influenced me. You were a man of few words and immediate actions. I remember the time you found something on the radio offensive, so you threw it through the kitchen window. And once when a neighbor's cat kept you awake, you shot it.

I also remember how the neighborhood teenagers would cower in your presence because you wanted to punch out any kid with a D.A. haircut. I hardly inspire such respect, either among my own kids or their friends. But I am doing something that is considered pretty bold in these kinder and gentler times.

This is going to be hard to grasp for someone who died in 1959: We've been paying thirty bucks a month to a TV station so our kids can watch people dressed like Detroit pimps. Well, I've had enough, and I've written a letter to the company that provides this service and asked that it be disconnected.

Aren't you proud?
—Jack
P.S. Your grandson wears an earring.

The bright side of back-to-school time: Kids are 1 year older

IT HAPPENS EVERY YEAR; MY KIDS go back to school. Basically, it's not a problem. One night they go to bed before the test pattern appears on local TV channels; they wake up the following morning, shake me down for lunch money and then leave for several hours to learn about global warming and politically correct thinking.

Each time school starts, it means that they are another year closer to supporting me in my old age. It's wonderful. I can't wait to put the arm on them for my blood pressure medication. "And while your at the drugstore, don't forget Metamucil, I've been kinda slow lately."

The declining years are tough, but they provide the only way to get even with succeeding generations.

While I welcome the first day of school, the preparation for it gives me deep stomach pains. "They need clothes," my wife says every year in early August.

"Let 'em wear what they wore last year," I say every August. It does little good: frau und kinder disappear for several days into the world of back-to-school sales. Clothes are only part of it. There's also school supplies. For generations kids have gone to school armed with only No. 2 pencils, loose-leaf paper and ball-point pens. Now there's a Trapper Keeper, which is to notebooks what computers are to typewriters. They are a must for grade school and junior high mouth-breathers, and they run almost five bucks. An anal retentive's dream, they are a notebook with a built-in closet organizer.

"We saved a lot of money hitting the outlet malls," my wife disclosed after an absence of several weeks.

"I got two rayon shirts," gushed the oldest during debriefing.

"Do they have to be dry cleaned?" I inquired in that how-much-more-can-this-cost voice that fathers always use when dealing with teen-age offspring.

"Yeah, they're rayon," he said as if explaining the concept of gravity to somebody with a very low ACT score.

"Can't you hand-wash them with Woolite?" I asked, exhibiting my knowledge of wonder fabrics.

"Yeah, right," his mother scowled. Later the kid drops the big one: "I'm a senior this year, and I can eat lunch off campus. We'll probably go to Portillo's every day."

"Just how do you plan to get there?" I asked.

"My friends have cars," he informed.

"Watch your cholesterol," I said. "The cheese fries are a killer, and I don't even want to think about those Italian beefs."

Some parents worry about their kid's involvement in a car accident. Others fear their progeny might fall in with Democrats. With me it's coronary bypass surgery necessitated by his steady diet of pizza, burgers and Coke Classic.

Not content with just warning him about heart disease, I decide to administer a sociology lecture: "And if the cops ever stop you, get rid of that earring."

"Why?" he asked.

"They hate guys who don't look normal," I said. "They'll pull you out of the car and hit you with nightsticks. Didn't you ever see movies of the '68 Democratic Convention?"

"I'm going to Portillo's," he said as he left.

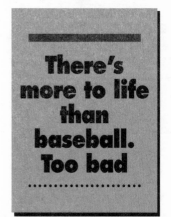

There's more to life than baseball. Too bad

IT'S STARTING AGAIN AND IT'S only February. We made the obligatory trip to Sportmart to try out aluminum bats; I always get nervous when I see the kid swing them in the aisles.

On Saturday I drove him and a friend to a place near Aurora where they stood in a batting cage for an hour to practice hitting pitched balls. "These pitching machines throw breaking balls, too," he told me.

I watched him as other kids came in with their middle-aged, big-stomached fathers who nodded at one another as if to say, "I don't know about you, but because our kids play ball, our lives are similar."

This week the kid will go to a team meeting at his high school. There will be a week of tryouts, then indoor practices begin. Nightly he'll tell me how his arm feels and of any new subtlety that he has picked up from the high school coaching staff.

When the weather gets better and the days a little longer, I'll hit fly balls to him and his younger brother in the evenings after work. The dog will go with us to the park across the street and chase the ball each time it's hit or thrown. Because he's older now, he begins to limp after half an hour. I sometimes carry him back to the house, then return to my duties with the fungo bat.

From time to time the kids laugh at me because I'm fat and I look stupid when I swing and miss. After a while I'm exhausted. "This is the last one," I tell them as I get ready to swing. It is never the last one.

By April, my oldest son will be playing baseball several times a week, with double-headers on Saturdays. On the way home from games, we always argue over his stats.

"I went three for four today," he tells me.

"Whaddaya mean? That grounder to left was an error on the shortstop," I say.

"He dove for it," he says.

"It rolled through his legs," I tell him. After games he pitches, we stop at a 7-Eleven store so I can buy him a cola Slurpee and a five-pound bag of ice to wrap around his arm.

There have been summers when I have not missed a single game. Each season, fewer of the regular parents show up; their kids eventually realize there are things in life other than baseball.

My ten-year-old son will begin playing in May. Supportive parents flock to the games in minivans, with aluminum lawn chairs and plastic coolers full of diet drinks.

"He's swinging late," my wife says about our kid's performance at the plate.

"Yeah, and he isn't rolling his wrists," I observe. Neither my wife nor I have ever played a single inning of baseball.

By July, my oldest son finishes all his regular games, but he extends his season with tournament teams. For a while we'll go to a game every night. Some players miss games because their families go on vacation, but real baseball parents wouldn't think of yanking their kid from a tournament to see plastic alligators at DisneyWorld.

In August, neighborhood kids get together daily to play whiffle ball. The game requires a long, thin plastic bat, bases and no other equipment. They store these things year-round in the window wells on the side of our house.

A week before school begins they have a tournament. Each team has kids from second grade through high school. They play for 8 and 10 hours a day, using my telephone between games to recruit extra players while they drink gallons of my bottled water.

"Dammit," I tell them. "Go outside and drink out of the hose."

"We're worried about radon," my ten-year-old says. Then school begins and it's over for another year. As they approach manhood, they, too, will eventually realize there's more to life than baseball.

I hope it isn't soon.

WORK

....

Pronouns are victims in battle of the sexes

....

"**Y**OU BOTCHED THIS editing," the office feminist told me as she adjusted her right shoulder pad.

"The sentence reads, 'Everyone is happy until he must choose.' What's wrong with that?" I asked.

"The pronoun 'he,'" she said.

"The word 'everyone' is singular," I gloated. "So it takes a singular pronoun." Editing is basically boring, but it's these little victories that keep you going.

"Please," she said. "I know that much. It's not a question of singular or plural but of sex."

I had her now. I keep a copy of Strunk and White's "The Elements of Style" with me at all times. I popped it open to page 60. "Hate to burst your bubble," I said. "But I'd just like to quote a few sentences from Strunk and White: 'The use of "he" as a pronoun for nouns embracing both genders is a simple, practical convention rooted in the beginnings of the English language. "He" has lost all suggestion of maleness in these circumstances.'"

Three years of carrying that book with me every minute had finally paid off. I had squashed her like a bug.

"You can't be serious," she laughed while adjusting her other shoulder pad. "Nobody uses Strunk and White anymore. It's outdated. Haven't you heard of genderless prose? The sentence should read, 'Everyone is happy until he or she must choose.' Using 'he or she' makes the sentence politically correct."

"What's the point?" I asked. She took a deep breath.

"The point is that men have dominated society long enough. Through language and customs they have denied women an access to power. How many women do you know who run a business?"

"I had an aunt who owned a bar on the South Side. She had access to power. She regularly bounced men who were twice her size."

"I'm talking about a big business like a major corporation."

"Look," I said. "It's only a pronoun. Whether we say 'he' or 'he or she' is not going to put a woman in charge of General Motors."

"Yes, but it is indicative of something much bigger. Now is the time to remove all traces of sexism from our language." She said the last sentence through clenched teeth.

I had noticed this "genderless prose" stuff before. My son recently brought home a note from his band director saying, "Every child should show up on time with his or her instrument." I never took "his" or "her" seriously, though. Working for a magazine owned by a white male who despises political correctness and who still doesn't use ZIP codes has protected me from these trends. My life has been a sheltered one.

But I wasn't about to give up with the office feminist. "Look," I said. "This 'his or her, he or she' thing is awkward. Isn't there some other way around it?"

"You could use the word 'one,' which is neither masculine nor feminine."

"It sounds too British," I said. "I've got a better idea, though. For hundreds of years haven't we used masculine pronouns whenever sex was unspecified?"

"Sad but true," she said.

"Then how about for the next five centuries if we use only feminine pronouns?"

"I like that," she smiled.

"I do too," I said. "Especially in the sentence, 'Anyone obsessed with sex in pronouns needs her head examined.'"

"Sit on your Strunk and White," she said in a very masculine voice.

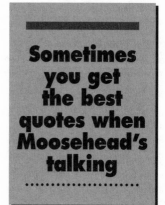

Sometimes
you get
the best
quotes when
Moosehead's
talking

I'VE DONE SOME HARD WORK IN my day. For a couple of years I labored as a dock worker loading trucks. I worked as a piano mover off and on for a good part of my life, and I even spent a summer as a greenhouse worker for the Chicago Park District.

The only problem was that I never got inside the greenhouse; I spent my days outside, hoeing a field of mums.

But a far as back-breaking labor goes, none of this compares with what I've just gone through. I started a couple of years ago on a book. Actually, it's not my creation, and my name doesn't even appear on it.

It's what is called a "tribute book." A guy who is outstanding in his field always has numerous friends and hangers-on who will write a letter on his behalf saying what a swell person he is and how much he has affected the lives of others or how he's been an inspiration to everybody around him—you get the idea.

One of The Great One's coat-holders then collects all these testimonials, has them edited, and gets The Great One to write a few words about how tough things used to be or how much he's enjoyed working with all the pathetic mopes who have written letters on his behalf. Finally, the book is published, and The Great One sells copies to his admirers.

I started on it as a part-time project. The Collector sent me forty letters that I was to edit. Basically, they fell into two categories.

"Dear Collector,

Thank you for asking me to write this. I first met The Great One when I was only 23. He gave me a warm handshake and put me at ease immediately..."

The letter then goes on for seven pages telling how wonderful The Great One is and how much everyone loves him.

The second type of letter was just as effusive in its praise but for a different subject.

"Dear Collector,

Thank you for asking me to write this. As you know I have a wonderful job and my life is pretty great because like The Great One, I too am wonderful... ." Eight pages are then dedicated to the accomplishments of the writer with only peripheral references to The Great One.

After editing 20 letters, I called The Collector. "Look," I said. "This book is boring. Can't you find somebody who hates this guy and who will write a letter about what a jerk he is?"

"No," The Collector said. "That's what makes The Great One so great, nobody has a bad word to say about him."

"OK," I said. "Then did he ever punch out his kids or make the walls shake in a sleazy motel with somebody other than his wife? We need more human interest stuff."

"The Great One lived an exemplary life..." After the letters were edited The Collector interviewed The Great One and sent me several hours of tapes. Here, The Great One loosened up a bit. When asked about someone he once worked for, he said, "That guy was the cheapest S.O.B. I ever met," and then went on to give several examples of just what a cheap S.O.B. the guy was.

I thought we had hit pay dirt. At least we had a decent blurb for the dust jacket.

Along with the tapes The Collector sent a picture of The Great One at the interview session. I counted eight empty Moosehead bottles on the table in front of him.

I transcribed fifty typewritten pages, which I then edited and sent to The Great One for his approval. Unfortunately, Moosehead was not present when he read them. He cut out all the interesting stuff, including "That guy was the cheapest S.O.B. I ever met."

The Great One's book was finally published in hardcover and sells for $18.95. Aside from the 40 complimentary copies sent to the contributors and the 100 or so that The Great One took for himself, eight books have been sold.

Cologne wars — scents vs. sense

MY GRANDMOTHER WORE Chanel No. 5 on special occasions, usually wakes. Combined with the ever-present scent of her pork roasts, it was pretty alluring.

My mother wore Chanel No. 5 too, but not with any regularity. Even so, it was the only scent I associated with women for most of my young life. Girls of the neighborhood dabbed on Avon products, "Here's My Heart" and others, but I never took those scents seriously and now cannot recall them.

The men in my family were into Old Spice after-shave exclusively, except for one uncle who was in sales. The outcast of the family wore Mennen Skin Bracer. He also wore jewelry, which my father despised.

It wasn't until I went away to college that I learned of colognes for men. "It's different than after-shave," my roommate instructed. "It really turns chicks on." I had to try it. I was having little luck with Old Spice.

"You smell like a babe," my grandfather told me when I arrived at home on semester break, sporting borrowed Canoe. I was deeply hurt. He doesn't know what it does to women, I thought. Probably a good thing.

In succeeding years I worked my way through a bottle or two of English Leather, Brut and a few scents I can no longer recall. My early 30s were my musk years.

Now I rarely wear any cologne or after-shave, even at wakes. About a year ago my wife gave me a bottle of Fahrenheit. "You smell like cucumbers," my youngest said every time I put it on. I don't wear it anymore. Who wants to remind people of Dominick's produce counter?

The best thing about colognes and perfumes are their sales campaigns. I like those dopey Calvin Klein commercials that are shot in black and white, where thin, severe-looking men and pouting women appear to be punishing one another. "Savor the essence," the announcer says just as the inmates finish another psychodrama. They always remind me of "Twin Peaks" except that none of the women wear eye patches or talk to logs.

The office where I work is in the throes of a cologne war. I don't know how it started but I remember that one day the hallways smelled of Laura Ashley.

"Who's wearing it?" I asked. "The new woman," somebody said.

Within a week things had accelerated. Every woman sported a different scent, one more intense than the next.

Even a few men got involved with a spritz or two of Chaps. The guys in shipping found their old bottles of Drakkar, which is pretty strong stuff that is advertised by a bare-chested male indulging in target archery. I don't understand the logic of it all, but it seems to sell.

I had a headache for the entire first week of the cologne war. Even so, I didn't retaliate by uncorking my bottle of Fahrenheit.

On Friday a middle-aged woman who works there showed up with an industrial-strength perfume. It's probably a mutation of the male Fahrenheit because it smells like watermelons—not just a few, a truckload—and fabric softener.

On Monday a male co-worker sported something reminiscent of naphtha. "What is it?" I asked.

"Egoiste," he said. "It's Chanel for men." The Egoiste ad reads, "To assume he is uncaring or aloof is to misread him. He walks on the positive side of that fine line separating arrogance from an awareness of self-worth."

I'm going to buy a bottle. I might have some wakes to attend.

Editors come and go — some do so diurnal

YESTERDAY WAS MY THIRD anniversary as a magazine editor. It's been interesting. The turnover rate in editorial is similar to that of most fast-food franchises. Nine fellow editors have come and gone during my three years.

No two were alike, and all came to work in editorial for different reasons. One woman was hired because the boss liked her attitude. "She's positive, a real go-getter," he told me.

She was. But she had never read a book and didn't have a clue as to how words went together. I knew we were in trouble when she asked, "What's a preposition?"

Her writing was a mess. "Try not to give the reader so much information all at once," others often told her.

"But I like the way it sounds this way. It's the real me," she said every time anyone suggested she toss in a couple of simple declarative sentences.

After exactly one month the real her was dumped. Her successor was equally whacked out, but in a different way. She had a master's degree in English and a grasp of grammar and punctuation but loved to throw in words nobody understood.

"I edited in the word 'diurnal' into this article," she said.

"What does it mean?" I asked. "You don't know what 'diurnal' means?" she repeated three times before going on. "It means occurring only in the daytime."

"But there's one little problem," I said. "The author of this manuscript is a jazz musician who grew up in Harlem in the 1930s. I don't think he uses words like 'diurnal.'"

"You mean he doesn't know the meaning of 'diurnal' either?" she asked, rolling her head from side to side as if the guy from Harlem and I were born without frontal lobes.

She was canned within three months and called a week after her departure. "I have a waitress job for the time being," she said.

"Is it diurnal or nocturnal?" I asked, but she didn't get it.

Working with nut cases is one thing, but working for a nut case can be depressing. For a year, I labored under a managing editor who was on a passive-voice search-and-destroy mission.

If I handed her a manuscript containing the sentence "during the Civil War, many drummer boys were shot," she would hand it back with the words "were shot" circled. "Who shot them?" she'd ask. "Please avoid passive voice by having the subject perform the action."

I would then rewrite the sentence to "During the Civil War, the enemy shot many drummer boys," which was stupid because the article was about drummer boys and not the enemy.

She once gave me a short blurb she wrote for the anniversary of Beethoven's birth. "Beethoven was born in 1770," was the first sentence, which I promptly rewrote to, "Beethoven's mother bore him in 1770." I attached a note with the standard, "Please avoid passive voice by having the subject perform the action." She didn't speak to me for several weeks.

Most of the editors I've worked with were women, but there was one guy whom I will always remember for his mastery of cliches. Editors usually remove them, but he substituted his favorites.

Editing a manuscript containing the hackneyed, "It's just water over the dam," he crossed out "over the dam" and put in "under the bridge." "I think we're through the woods on this one," usually became "I can see the light at the end of the tunnel."

After eight months he received two weeks' severance pay and headed for greener pastures.

Laughing in the face of economic ruin

I'VE HEARD THE QUESTION A million times in the past few weeks. "You didn't really quit your job in this economy, did you?"

"Yes," I tell them. "That's exactly what I did. Walked out and kept going. No two weeks' notice, no farewell party, just my big butt heading south out the door."

This is followed by the inevitable "Why?" which is followed by the inevitable "Whatya gonna do now?"

"Beats me," I say to the last question, but the "why" is easy—because I despise work of all kinds. I always have. It gives me low self-esteem and dandruff.

Even though the economy is belly-up, I had to go. "I've never seen you look worse," a friend told me just before I walked. Regular money has that effect on me.

My departure from magazine editing after only three years shocked my fellow employees. "I thought you'd be here for life," one of them said. "But you've finally learned when to use 'compared with' as opposed to 'compared to,'" another offered. "You can't quit now."

It didn't matter. I left on Veterans Day, which was apropos because I was the only person in the company ever to scrub urinals for the military. Kinda gives me goose bumps when I think about it.

Even though my time was up, it was tough to leave. Recently promoted to managing editor, I began wearing a watch and had my shirts professionally laundered. More that once I caught myself staring at a pair of wingtips at the local shoe store, and sometimes I would peruse copies of *Money* magazine at the library. I greased my hair straight back and carried a Mont Blanc pen. I even fantasized about trading in my Festiva for a Ford Escort with a tape deck.

This was life in the fast lane; at least for me it was. "You've finally arrived," my mother told me after observing that my slacks were a better grade of polyester.

But in the end, I knew this job wasn't permanent. The managing editor I replaced lasted a matter of weeks. "I'll give you four months in this job," she said to me as she headed out the door for the last time.

I lasted six, but for the last two, the publisher, a dour man who listened incessantly to Bruckner symphonies and who forbade the use of ZIP codes on company correspondence, didn't speak to me. I guess my predecessor was right; four months was about it.

My last day there was uneventful. I drank coffee, edited a manuscript or two and ate three bags of microwave popcorn. The publisher ignored me, still angry over an argument we had eight weeks earlier in which he accused me of never working between 10 p.m. and midnight. I'm not making this up.

Rather than let the thing be, I called his secretary. "Is Daddy withholding his love today?" I asked each morning of his silence.

That may have been a mistake on my part, but these things happen in the workplace. Few people find lasting happiness and satisfaction there. Those who do were probably dropped by baby sitters.

"This job will probably make me get organized or kill me," I said after my first week as managing editor. I guess I was successful in that it did neither.

As for what to do next, I don't want to think about it. I'm on vacation.

Job wanted: hard worker, experience with parking lots

IT IS NOW TWO MONTHS SINCE I walked out of my last full-time job. No regrets. Since my departure I've picked up a few bucks writing, worked as a temporary editor and went on a week-long vacation.

But now the vacation is over. My kid starts college next September, and it would be humiliating to have his father's occupation listed as aluminum can recycler.

But worse than my kid's humiliation is my own. How can I have any sense of self-worth unless I commute two hours a day and spend at least forty hours a week in wingtips?

I've scoured the help-wanted ads regularly but haven't found anything. The problem is that most jobs require enthusiasm. "The successful candidate will possess strong communications skills, conceptual thinking/interpersonal skills as well as the desire to be part of a dynamic team."

I've got strong communication skills—can write memos with the best of them. And as far as conceptual thinking/interpersonal skills, I have no equal. Just last week I entered the Fire Bell Pub with only two dollars in my pocket, and because of my superior interpersonal skills and my ability to conceptualize, I glommed on to a couple of visiting academics and sustained myself on successive pitchers of Moosehead, which they bought.

What scares me about the above ad is "The desire to be part of a dynamic team." Probably a bunch of guys with shiny chins and songsheets who hustle Amway on the side. No thanks.

No job search would be complete without a resume, which is a single sheet of paper that gives the salient points of your professional career while showing off the different typefaces of your laser printer.

I wrote my resume the day after I left my last job. And I've written successive resumes each day since.

Every time I've showed one of my friends, they suggest I rework it. "Bury the part about the Chavez lettuce boycott but play up the fact that you've worked as a parking lot attendant. It shows you have a mind for details."

All resumes require an accompanying cover letter, something that will capture a potential employer's interest:

Dear Sir or Madam, I saw your ad in the Sunday Tribune for a professional cow slaughterer and bung puller. I have spent my life in slaughter houses. *Silence of the Lambs* is my favorite movie. Enclosed is my resume.

Regards,

J.Z.

Despite sparkling cover letters, I've yet to get an interview, which is depressing. At times it seems the entire world is going to work, except for me. I often stand at my back door early in the morning and wave to neighbors as they drive toward the Eisenhower. "Hope you write a good report today," I yell in an effort to encourage them. Sometimes I shout, "Good luck with Lotus 1-2-3," to accountants who pass by.

Luckily, I have a historical perspective on the whole employment picture. The idea of having a job, a place to go each day where it's warm and people smell good, didn't exist until the Industrial Revolution. Before that, everybody just hung out.

In fact, there are still primitive Amazon tribesmen who do not work a 40-hour week so that at 65 they can enjoy free blood-pressure screening and discounts on Players' Club memberships. Instead they while away their productive years eating fresh fruit and having sex.

Fortunately though, we live in an industrialized society. Here we balance 40-plus-hour work weeks with leisure pursuits such as playing golf, watching talk shows and drinking protein-powder milkshakes.

Pass the avocados, please.

Doubts start to sprout as the interview looms

FRIDAY AFTERNOON THE PHONE rings. Probably my kid wanting a ride. "Mr. Zimmerman?" Uh-oh, somebody hustling replacement windows.

"Yeah, this is Jack Zimmerman."

"I'm calling about THE JOB. We'd like to get you down here on Monday for an interview."

OK, Zimmerman, don't sound too eager. "Let me check my book."

I don't even own a book. I write appointments on loose-leaf paper, which I stick to the refrigerator with a magnet. But I like the way "Let me check my book" sounds.

"What time on Monday?" I ask. *Zimmerman, you have 24 hours free that day. You've been out of work since November.*

"Three OK with you?" the voice on the phone says.

"I think I can move a few things around and be there at 3." *Zimmerman, you have one thing to do next week: take your mother shopping.*

I grab a fresh piece of loose leaf paper, write "THE JOB—3 on Monday," and fasten it to the refrigerator with a magnet from my insurance agent.

"They called. I have a job interview on Monday," I tell the wife. "Yes! Yes! Yes! Yes!" she yells. Likewise the kids. They high-five one another.

What to wear? "Blue blazer, grey slacks, that striped shirt with the button-down collar and your art-deco tie," the wife says.

"Can't do it," I tell her. "Job interviews require a white shirt."

"You have white shirts, don't you?" I check the closet. There's one white shirt. It has ink on the right sleeve, but I'm wearing a blazer.

Should have a suit for this but don't own one. Got fat and gave them to Purple Heart Veterans. No big deal. They were blue serge jobs from Robert Hall.

Saturday I get a haircut. "Got a job interview," I tell the barber. "Wanna look good." I'm in the barber chair and realize I didn't turn on the answering machine.

Who cares? I have an interview. If I get the job, the answering machine goes the way of the blue serge suits.

Sunday I'm on the couch all day. Watch John Wayne in *The Shootist*. Then basketball, which I hate.

"You haven't moved from that couch all day," the wife says. "I'm mentally preparing for the interview," I tell her. I think about my father. He worked his entire life, had several high-paying jobs and never took an interview. When did all this interview stuff start?

I go to bed at 8 on Sunday night. Monday I'm up at 7 and have several hours to kill. Wife and kids are gone. Start rewriting my novel. Quit at 11:30. Make pasta, fry peppers. No garlic salt this time! Interview is only a few hours away.

Get dressed. Wish I were 30 pounds thinner. Wonder if I'll be the fattest person there. Was at my last job.

Take the train downtown. Get to the office 40 minutes early. Better go to the bathroom. I can't spend 40 minutes in a bathroom, they'll think I'm weird. Go to a record store first. Kill only 15 minutes in the bathroom.

Stand in front of the mirror. Little specks of lint on blazer. Skin looks dry. Jeez, wish I had a moisturizer. Too late now.

Wait a minute. I wore that dumb cap all day. Now I have a ring across my forehead. "He's had brain surgery," they'll say. Get a paper towel and try to rub it away. No good. Now I have an inflamed ring on my forehead. Forget it. Go to the receptionist. "I'm here," I tell her.

I wait. Editorial position. When to use "between" and when to use "among"—no problemo. But what about "compared to" and "compared with"? Can't remember the rule.

"They'll see you now, Mr. Zimmerman." What if they don't like this tie? Feet look big in these shoes. I'm fat. There's ink on my right...

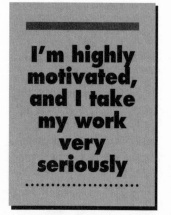

I'm highly motivated, and I take my work very seriously

JOB INTERVIEW. "COME IN," SHE says and shakes my hand. *Hope my breath is OK. What about the dandruff on my glasses? Too late now—we're off and running.*

She leans back in her chair the way executives do. "So tell me, why do you want to work for this company?"

Because I need a job and I'm tired of shutting off the exhaust fan whenever I go to the bathroom so I don't miss a phone call. Wait, I can't say that. I need something broad and general.

"I've always admired the contributions made by this company and feel that I could work here."

Hey Zimm, not bad for the first question.

"Yes, but you don't even know what this job entails."

Uh-oh, she's getting technical. And I've only been in here three minutes. Tell her the truth: You want a place to hang out so you can knock off another novel.

"The actual duties really don't matter that much to me. The important thing is that working here would give me a place to excel."

You're laying it on a little thick, Zimm. Watch it, you might wind up in sales.

She opens a desk drawer. "Read this job description and I'll answer any questions you might have."

OK, Zimm, you're too nervous to read, so just scan the page looking for the words scrub and urinals close together. Why do I keep hearing "The Flintstone Theme" played by an alto sax? Flintstones, we're the Flintstones, we're a page right out of his-tor-ee. Don't waste time singing along. Scan the job description. Scrub and urinals aren't there!

"Everything looks fine to me. I have no questions."

Wait a minute, Zimm. What about this "maintain files"? You'll screw up big time. Most days you can't find your car keys.

"Is that street musician bothering you?"

That's what it is. Some guy hustling pin money eight floors below. Maybe I should tell her I have a recording of Carl Fontana playing the same tune.

"I've tried to have him arrested, but the police can't do anything."

Better skip the bit about Carl.

"What do you think is your best attribute?"

Tell her how funny you are. Tell her about your last job; how you threw parties whenever the boss was out of town and how everybody got so loaded they couldn't punch in the secret code to turn on the alarm system when they left the building. "I'm highly motivated and I take my work very seriously." *Flintstones, we're the ...*

"Why did you leave your last job?"

My boss was nuts. Show her the company stationery and envelopes with no ZIP codes. Go ahead, you've got it in your valise. And tell her how he wouldn't allow editors to use computers. Tell her how he sometimes played with a remote-controlled submarine in the company swimming pool. "I felt that I had stopped growing and wanted an opportunity to advance professionally."

Jeez, that Flintstone tune is giving me a headache. Can't somebody buy that guy a fake book so he learns something new?

She stands up and extends her hand. I guess it's over. "I'll make my final decision within three weeks."

That's another 21 days without the bathroom exhaust fan.

Say something funny like "yabba dabba doo!"

"Thank you, I really enjoyed the interview," I tell her.

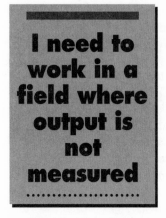

I need to work in a field where output is not measured

I'VE BEEN AT THE JOB SEARCH thing again. Actually, I've moved from seeking out the one perfect employment situation that would be fulfilling and challenging, to just finding a job.

But just any job isn't good enough. Tomorrow I could start at a firm that is in the forefront of asbestos removal. But the exposure to asbestos could cause large polyps to form on the backs of my eyeballs, or worse—asbestos removal could addle my brain, causing me to spend my declining years in the Peruvian jungle with a 22-year-old physical therapist named Big Mary.

Until now I've been looking for employment in all the wrong places.

I've considered teaching jobs. I'd love to stand in front of a high school English class, explaining the difference between "continuous" and "continual." But I don't have a teaching certificate, and aside from winning strategies at Trivial Pursuit and knowing how to cadge drinks from strangers, there isn't much I could teach. Actually, I never learned the difference between "continuous" and "continual." "Use 'It happens a lot,'" I'd say.

I've also considered going into management. The newspaper is full of management positions, but the fact that I can't find my car keys on two successive mornings tells me that I really shouldn't be in charge of the affairs of others.

For a time I thought about selling real estate. But that requires a lot of hours on weekends and a big, glitzy car. My Ford Festiva won't cut it, even though I recently cleaned the upholstery.

Besides, I might hit it big, sell a few houses, and then my picture would appear in a real estate ad as "Salesman of the Month" and former creditors would show up with their palms extended. All sales jobs carry a lot of pressure to perform. I'm looking for something with no pressure, just a place to hide so I can finish another novel while making a few bucks. I need to work in a field where output isn't measured.

That's why I've chosen law. The legal profession is the perfect place for me. For several years I worked for a lawyer who, when asked a simple question, would stare off into the distance while sucking on the earpiece of his eyeglasses.

"The first thing a good lawyer does is gather all the facts," he said.

"Look," I said. "Mr. Important Person is at O'Hare and needs a ride here. Should I pick him up or tell him to take a cab?"

"Do we really want to be a common carrier? And does Mr. Important Person expect us to reimburse him if he has to pay for a cab? Would the goodwill generated by you picking him up be worth the lost time at work? Do you have a reading on what kind of treatment he expects?"

My former boss would then ask several more pithy questions while Mr. Important Person stood at an O'Hare pay phone waiting for a call from us.

We would never make that call. Eventually my boss would say, "The study of law teaches one to think clearly, and what this problem needs is clear thinking."

He'd then shuttle me out of his office so he could clear-think in private while sucking on his glasses some more.

After standing around O'Hare for a while, Mr. Important Person took care of his own transportation and refused to ever again have anything to do with my boss or me.

Somehow my boss's company survived these episodes. After each one, my boss would say, "Clear thinking is the answer," and then lean back in his leather chair and attack his glasses again.

And he wasn't a legal lightweight who went to night school for a law degree. He was a graduate of Yale.

If he can do it, so can I. I'm going to clear-think with the best of them. That's why I began my legal training on Monday.

My glasses are shorter already.

Final trip over the edge is often well-supervised

FOR A FEW YEARS I WORKED AT a place where everyone was over-paid. It wasn't a matter of a couple of bucks each payday. We were paid 50 percent more than people doing comparable work at other companies.

There was one problem, though. The boss was nuts. Of course, nobody realized this for at least a month after being hired. But then the boss, who was also the owner of the company, called the new employee into his office and the games would begin.

"I want you to take this manuscript, edit it, transcribe the cassette tapes and integrate them into the manuscript and wind up with a book when you're done," he told me a month after I started. "But I don't want you to do this on company time. Do it on weekends or after work."

He had given me the big assignment on a Friday. On Monday, I was back in his office. "I didn't see you here this weekend," he said.

"That's because I wasn't here this weekend," I told him.

"How long is that book going to be?" he asked.

"Beats me," I said. "I have no idea, especially since I never did this before."

He then told me the importance of working on weekends because "that's when the real work gets done." He also kept badgering me for the number of pages the assigned book was supposed to be.

"Somebody has to put a dot on the wall so we have something to aim at," he repeated several times that afternoon. But because he was the owner of the company and had worked there since he was a boy, he was better equipped to put a dot on the wall, or so I thought. Besides, it was his wall. He only smiled when I told him this and then repeated the question on the book's total pages.

To make the episode worse, he played a Bruckner symphony on his office stereo. During the scherzo movement I cracked. "The book will be 162 pages long," I told him, pulling the number out of the air. I just wanted to go home.

This was the way the game was played there. Two or three weekends a month I showed up for work, so I could be seen by the boss, then headed home. Eventually I stayed each night until 6:30 or 7:00 so I could put dots on walls. Finally, after three years and all nine Bruckner symphonies, I left for good.

"You'll never make that kind of money again," others who stayed said.

It didn't matter. If I stayed, I would have killed the boss. I was having a recurring dream in which I removed parts of his body with a belt sander. Normally, I'm a placid soul, but three years with a nut case and Anton Bruckner nearly drove me over the edge. And had I indulged my fantasy, I'd be on the evening news, my co-workers would be interviewed, and psychologists would talk about my early toilet-training. High school friends would tell reporters that I was different — every aspect of my life would be examined.

But nobody would investigate my boss, the guy who spent three years driving me over the edge. And that's the way the media are handling the recent post office murder and mayhem.

Yes, these killers were unbalanced souls who spent too much time watching "The Terminator." And yes, people like them should not have access to sharp objects, much less semiautomatic weapons; and yes, their violent behavior probably has its roots in some childhood trauma. But just once I'd like to see the lives of their immediate supervisors examined closely.

Maybe they listened to Bruckner symphonies and put dots on walls.

Hemingway would never have made it in PR

I WROTE MY FIRST PRESS RELEASE this week. This after knocking out a thousand newspaper columns, a novel and several short stories. I had hoped to escape life without ever typing the words "For Immediate release." No deal.

My PR career spanned five months and two days when the boss announced that each department member would have to pen a couple of press releases for an upcoming monster release. The monster release involved embossed folders, plenty of 8-by-10 glossies and a ton of laser-printed prose. It made my scalp itch.

Nobody had noticed that I had slipped by all these months without writing a single release. It was like pitching several innings of a no-hitter. Every night I went home, looked in the bathroom mirror and said, "Well, Zimmerman, you've pulled it off for another day."

Of course, I wasn't a complete novice with press releases. Early in my writing career I tried to imitate humor columnist Dave Barry, so I knew how to use my computer's caps lock.

FOR IMMEDIATE RELEASE — IMPORTANT PERSON ANNOUNCES IMPORTANT STUFF!

Important Person and longtime associate of Very Important Person today announced his support for the recent changes in the management structure of the blah, blah, blah... "This breakthrough will allow us to serve our public even better than before. It is an important step for the blah, blah, blah..." said Important Person.

It took me 52 hours to finish both releases. "Is this how Important Person wants this positioned?" the Boss asked when I handed her my first release after only 90 minutes of writing.

"Beats me," I said. "I never talked to Important Person. He's very busy, so I made up all of this." She looked at me for a long time, then took the afternoon off.

Nobody ever told me press releases are supposed to be

grounded in fact. Even the company's employee handbook doesn't mention it. What's the point of writing if you can't make up stuff? Hemingway would never have made it in PR.

FOR IMMEDIATE RELEASE
Francis Macomber was happy. He had a short life. "It was good," he said at Thursday's press conference.

Hardly the level of modern corporate communications.

Anyway, at the urging of my boss I called Important Person, got his input, then sent him a FAX of the release. And when that was done, two or three people inputted some more. After several revisions and inputs, the first release was finished and printed. The second one followed a few days later. Only two people inputted on it, so it didn't take very long. Then I asked for a week of vacation, but I'm not eligible until I've been in the job for a year.

The hard part about writing press releases is getting motivated. The truth is, except for PR types, no one has ever read a press release. In my last job as a magazine editor I received daily shipments of press packages. I'd go through them, save any 8-by-10 glossies of Paula Abdul or Anne-Sophie Mutter and toss everything else. None of the information contained in the press packages ever made it to print, unless my eye caught a release that had an extraordinary number of consecutive hyphenated adjectives: "Sneer Corporation announced the development of a hand-held, voice-activated, self-contained, low-cost Whoozitz." I've always been a sucker for hyphenated modifiers.

A month ago I had lunch with a major New York PR legend. "Who in your office writes the press releases?" I asked. "Our agency doesn't use them," he said. "When we want to place something in a paper or a magazine, we schmooze the editor, you know — take him out to lunch and pitch the story."

This I could handle.

Cold sweats among the tonsorially challenged

"**D**ID YOU SEE THE STORY in the paper?" the woman in the next office asked. "No," I said. "But I heard about it."

"Things look bad for you. Better watch it," she said as she patted the top of my head. Later another fellow employee left a newspaper clipping on my desk. "Study links baldness, heart disease," was the headline.

According to the accompanying chart that contained sketches of different degrees of male baldness, I should have been dead four years ago. Unfortunately, I manifest the symptoms of every disease I read about. The rest of the day was spent alone in my office performing yoga breathing techniques and chanting an occasional mantra in hopes of warding off the big one.

That's the way my day went, and probably the way the day went for every bald guy in America. Such is the price of receding hairlines.

It wasn't until this morning that I realized the study that had caused cold sweats among this country's tonsorially challenged had a major flaw. Men with toupees were not studied.

Not a single researcher said, "Hey, check out the heart attack statistics among guys who wear rugs and guys who have individual hair follicles drilled into their noggins. And while we're at it, let's study a few bald guys who grow long hair on one side and then comb it over the top."

Had researchers done these things, they would have found that hair impersonators are in the same low risk heart attack category as the natural mop heads.

The real reason for increased heart attacks among bald men has nothing to do with testosterone levels or lack of good or too much bad cholesterol. Bald guys have more heart problems because of a loser self-image. Society is so down on them that eventually they head for that big bottle of Minoxidil in the sky.

My baldness and image problems began in grade school.

"You've got a widow's peak," a girl at my eighth-grade dance said. "That means you'll go bald."

My heart sank. I had just completed eight years of Catholic schooling where they taught us that Christ had hair, and Pontius Pilate didn't.

I could have told her, "Yeah, I'll probably go bald and you'll probably have twenty kids and twenty different sets of stretch marks and you'll be married to a goon who removes ear wax with car keys and who never listens to Mozart." But I didn't say anything because my eight years of Catholic grade school trained me in being a gentleman, and a gentleman is one who never offends, even if he is bald.

High school was worse. "You have a receding hairline," girls told me. In my sophomore year my mother took me to a doctor to see if anything could be done. "But nobody else on either side of the family is bald," she said after the examination offered little help. The doctor, who had blond curls like Gorgeous George, told us I would have to live my life with an oversized forehead.

"Nothing can be done," he said shaking his head.

"I'm so sorry," my mother said in the same tone she used when I wasn't accepted by Chicago Teachers College because of low high school English grades.

In my late twenties, I went from going bald to being bald. And those with hair, especially women, never passed up a chance to comment. "Must get awful cold up there," a female co-worker said the other morning as she looked at my hairless expanse.

"Not as cold as that big fat tundra butt of yours," I wanted to say but didn't because I am a bald gentleman who never offends.

HOLIDAYS, VACATIONS, AND OTHER EVENTS

••••••••••••••••••••••

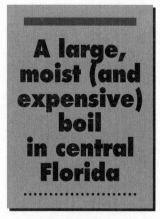

A large, moist (and expensive) boil in central Florida

••••••••••••••••

SOMEWHERE IT IS WRITTEN IN the scriptures that Disneyfication is essential to childhood. This means every kid and parent in the universe should visit the sacred city of Disney, near Orlando, Florida, to see Walt's view of creation.

To be one of the Disney faithful isn't cheap. These days a one-day ticket to Disney World runs over $30 per person, or $120 for a family of four. I've bought suits for less.

And packing the entire family off to Orlando, a large, moist boil in central Florida that resembles the Dells or Bartertown from *Beyond Thunderdome,* isn't cheap either. Air fares, motel rooms, meals, and a rental car can run as much as a down payment on a summer home. And let's not forget the obligatory Mickey T-shirt or baseball cap, both of which put a hole in $10.

Of course, I knew these things before leaving for Orlando, but what the hey, isn't life just one big cost overrun?

My relationship with Orlando predates Disney. Before Walt and the boys drained the first bucket of swamp water from central Florida, my grandfather was living near Orlando. When told of the plans for the Disney theme park, Gramps could only say, "These bozos expect people to come from all over the country to look at Mickey and Goofy? Do they think we're stupid?"

Twenty-five years later his grandsons and family stood in line 48 minutes for a jungle safari boat ride, along which plastic elephants spray one another with water while the boat pilot delivers a comedic dialogue: "Before we get under way, this side of the boat say 'Oooooo," and this side say 'Aaahhhh.' We'll be using that later!'"

The wait was tolerable in that the line zig-zagged through a maze of railings, which gave the impression that you were always moving, even though actual forward progress was minimal. They also played some Sidney Bechet records to give the ride a 1920s ambience.

Things got better, though. We waited only thirty-six minutes to see the haunted mansion but without Sidney Bechet. And the line for Space Mountain was under forty minutes.

Of course, no trip to the world of Walt is complete without at least a day spent at EPCOT, which stands for something like Environmental Whoosits of Whatsits and has a lot to do with the future of the earth as seen by Walt.

"You have to see EPCOT!" adults always gush after having returned from there.

I've seen it. The gardening is nice. Walt owns some dandy lawn edgers. But EPCOT reminds me of those clunky trade shows that General Motors used to truck around the country in the 1950s. They had names like "Futurama" and showed how well off we would be in just a few years when we'd have helicopters to commute to work in.

The problem is that everybody takes EPCOT way too seriously. In an entire day of viewing the future according to Walt, I did not see a single adult or child smile.

Hey, lighten up everybody. It's not the Stalin five-year plan. Walt and the boys are only cartoonists. They made up all this stuff. This isn't real science any more than the elephants on the jungle safari ride are real. Hydroponics will not feed the world and scientists cannot be miniaturized to the size of a single cell and shot into the bloodstream of a patient to observe healing.

One night we watched Walt's fireworks and laser light show. The woman standing next to me was from a small village near London, England. "We're spending our entire holiday here," she confided.

"Why?" I asked. "Because we love everything American," she said. Gramps should be here, I thought.

You invite the man in, but hope he leaves

HE SHOWED UP AT MY HOUSE the week before Christmas. I was writing in the dining room and watched him hobble up the front walk, carrying a shoulder bag full of stuff and limping badly. He handed me a business card when I opened the door. "Chicago Handicap something or other," it said.

"You interested in any pot holders or oven mitts? Maybe a broom?" he asked, talking out of the side of his mouth as if he were letting me in on a special deal.

I had him come in so I didn't have to stand in the doorway. I was still coughing from the flu.

"How much are the oven mitts?" I asked. "Seven bucks," he said as he sat across from me at the table.

It seemed a little steep, but I thought the guy probably needed seven bucks more than I did, so I handed him the money. He was still cold and blew on his hands. He didn't have gloves.

"My supervisor is supposed to pick me up outside in a few minutes. Mind if I sit here?"

"Make yourself at home," I told him, but I didn't really mean it. I wished he would go.

He lit a cigarette, which I wished he didn't do. But he looked as if he had paid his dues. Aside from his leg, he had some problem with his back that made his body always appear twisted.

He used the bathroom and came back to the table to smoke another cigarette. I could see my kids look in on us from time to time. They had that "Oh God, don't make me talk to him" look that suburban kids get when they see somebody who's on the skids.

"So how's business?" I finally asked after he finished the second cigarette, hoping he wouldn't start a third.

"Bad," he said. "It's tough to hustle this year. Nobody wants anything and everybody is mad. My girlfriend and I did a couple of condos last night and somebody called the cops on us. My girl-friend has a bum ticker, and I was gettin' worried."

"You gotta watch those condo owners," I told him. He laughed a little.

"What's your name?" I finally asked. "Danny," he said, pointing to his plastic-covered photo ID.

He didn't offer his last name and my eyes weren't good enough to read the ID, but it didn't matter.

He coughed frequently — one of those boozy, airy coughs that guys have who hit the Chesterfields and John Barleycorn pretty hard. When he asked me for a glass of water, I was careful to find a disposable glass. "The others are in the dishwasher," I told him.

Despite his problems, his face was clear and like a little kid's. I wondered what he was like when he was young and how he wound up walking around my neighborhood a few days before Christmas hustling oven mitts that people bought so he would leave them alone.

A van pulled up outside. "There's the boss," he said as he untwisted his body from the chair and headed for the door.

"You and your family have a merry Christmas," he said. "You too," I said closing the door behind him.

"What's this?" my wife later asked as she inspected the oven mitt on the dining room table.

"My Christmas present to myself," I said.

Here's a holiday rap to kick off shopping lunacy

BECAUSE THE DAY AFTER Thanksgiving is the official start of Christmas shopping idiocy, we at the Loose Change All-Night Existentialist Bookstore and Liposuction Clinic thought it apropos to kick off the season with something that would inspire you through the coming weeks of adversity, bedlam and lunacy.

Hard to believe that in less than 30 days we'll all be broke and depressed.

Anyway, we've stayed up quite late recent nights inhaling large amounts of oven cleaner while composing "The Loose Change Christmas Rap":

Attention, this is your director. Please form two lines, with the men-folk stage right and the women-folk stage left. Rapmaster, front and center, everybody clap on two and four, men-folk all together now...

> *Oooo, aaaah, ooooo,aaahhhhh... .*
> *We're not rich and we're not greedy,*
> *We want to buy stuff for our sweetie.*
> *She likes Chanel and Frango Mints,*
> *Burberry trench coats and Erte prints.*
> *Our kids want Walkmans they can take in the shower,*
> *And those dopey shoes from Eddie Bauer.*
> *If we only had time to sit and relax,*
> *Contemplate life without Sansabelt slacks,*
> *BMWs and Mont Blanc pens,*
> *Rolex watches and Mercedes Benz.*
> *Ooooo, aaaahhh, oooooo, aaaaah... .*

Not bad, men-folk. some of you guys look pretty silly in those leotards, though. Now it's your turn, ladies. Is the room this crowded or are most of you wearing shoulder pads? Rapmistress, a little brighter tempo puleeez...

It's not the gift but the thought that counts,
But we'd like him to think in large amounts.
Perhaps a fur or a brand new Audi,
Dinner at Spiaggia when we're feeling dowdy.
It's his gift though that we worry about,
He's always been a little too stout.
If he lost some weight he'd look so swell,
He's been stuck forever in 2 XL.
Ooooo, aaaahhh, oooo, aaahh... .

Very good, ladies. Now can we have the men-folk and women- folk join hands center stage and do the final verse together? You know, the one about the universal greediness of kids. Bring the house lights down, puleeez. Rapmaster, Rapmistress, are you ready?

Nintendo games and Nike shoes,
Skateboards, slot cars and Moody Blues;
Stereo Headphones and ZZ Top.
Compact discs, does it ever stop?
We got them clothes from the Gap,
Stone-washed jeans we plan to wrap;
Banana Republic, Marshall Field,
J.C. Penney, we shop with zeal.

Sorry to interrupt when you were doing so well, but it's hard to understand the words if your teeth are clenched. Try to loosen up on the final couple of lines...

Things were easier years ago,
Our folks were broke and had no dough.
Hard to believe when we were tykes,
We rode all day on one-speed bikes.
Then it happened, we all got married,
Now deep in debt we're always buried.

Bravo, Rappers; you are now ready to commence Christmas shopping. Remember, take no prisoners and pay cash if possible.

Scientific fact: Men lack shopping gene

I T'S THAT TIME OF YEAR AGAIN. The annual spending orgy is about to hit high gear.

According to psychologists quoted in the Trib's Tempo section and other professional journals, some men have a problem with gift giving. They say it has to do with toilet training. Which is why we have psychologists—so the rest of us don't have to deal with disgusting childhood concepts.

Anyway, any real man will tell you, the tough part of Christmas is not giving gifts but shopping for them.

If I had a closet full of wrapped presents, I would have no problem distributing them to others, even if the others were my in-laws. It's going to the mall and getting that all-day headache that makes me wish I were kidnapped the Friday after Thanksgiving and returned to my family on New Year's Eve.

But I've learned to deal with it. And for those of you who break into the shakes upon the arrival of the Lands' End Christmas catalog that shows up sometime in October, I offer a few shopping tips to make life easier.

If you are a married man who has not started Christmas shopping yet, do not panic; there's still time.

Coded into the genes of every male is the desire to provide for his loved ones. In the beginning we were the hunters and gatherers. Which means we have a primal urge to give those we love large, expensive offerings like dead mastodons or 46-inch projection televisions.

But large, expensive offerings don't cut it anymore. This is the 90s, a time for sensitive, caring men to give sensitive, caring gifts. Besides, we're broke and many of us are out of work.

Even when I was employed, I often waited until Dec 23 and then blew hundreds of dollars on a gift for my wife, only to receive the cold shoulder from her on Christmas morning. The year I gave her a roto-tiller is a perfect example.

Even the year I gave her a 30-gallon air compressor and tossed in a set of jumper cables as a token gift, coldness and indifference reigned.

But then I discovered an important principle of gift giving—at least as far as women are concerned. Whether you give them something big or small, they loathe anything useful.

If you think your wife or significant other really wants a Craftsman Wet/Dry Shop Vac, think again. Yes, it's only $90, and it comes with a gaggle of attachments, and it's just the ticket for sucking up household spills or gasoline seepage from nearby storage tanks.

Too bad it doesn't convey the Christmas spirit in the way that a little Oscar de la Renta Eau de Toilette ($48 at Carson's) does, or say "Merry Christmas" the same way that a pair of diamond earrings do.

But there is a way around this. Give her the Craftsman Wet/Dry Shop Vac with a 3.25-horsepower motor and 16-gallon capacity, but include with it a little love note that conveys your deep feelings for both her and the Christmas season. It doesn't have to be anything profound like Shakespeare or Stephen King, but it should be touching. I've included an example you can clip and tape on the top of the vacuum or the bag of extra filters, just in case you're not a literary type.

> Dearest,
> The winds of our love blow strong, just like this 3.25-horsepower vacuum that will suck up the mess after my next poker party.
> Merry Christmas,
> Poopsie

Timely tips for Christmas gifts

ALTHOUGH I CAN'T STAND Christmas and eagerly await the 26th of December so I can exchange useless gifts for a tank of nitrous oxide, my readers feel otherwise.

So, for the hordes of Christmas faithful who read this column, it's time for Loose Change Christmas gift suggestions.

Gifts for the male of the species:

Every man sees himself as some sort of Mr. Fixit. But when it comes to work around the house, most guys are hopelessly inept and can't complete the simplest do-it-yourself project without eventually hiring a flannel-shirted ya-hoo in a pickup truck to straighten things out.

Forget all that stupid stuff like cordless electric screwdrivers or magnetic stud finders—he'll only hurt himself. Instead, give the poor mope something he'll never forget, a sampler of herbal teas and a new set of snow tires.

But if all this is too steep and you were thinking of something more personal like cologne, stop! The only guys who wear that stuff raise house plants and put sparkle dust in their hair.

Give him some Old Spice or Mennen aftershave. If he doesn't like either scent, a little WD-40 applied after the morning face-scraping should be just the ticket.

Gifts for the lady in your life:

A woman is impossible to buy for, especially if you are married to her. She always wants something romantic like one of those dumb lace camisoles, but afterward, when you suggest she wear it, she reminds you that the gutters haven't been cleaned for six months.

A kitchen disposal is the answer. She'll think of you every time she uses it. And when the kids are bored with their video games, they can toss large objects into the sink and play with the reset button.

But wait! Maybe you're not married and the woman in your life has not undergone those hormonal changes that make her crave short hair, polyester dresses, vertical blinds and a Volvo.

Well, mister, you're in luck! Get a hold of a Frederick's of Hollywood catalog, a case of Beaujolais and I'll leave the rest to your imagination.

Gifts for Children:

Kids have too much. Ninety percent of the junk they were given last Christmas is broken or was sold at a garage sale in August. But there is a way around this. Select long-lasting, educational toys they can use well into adulthood like a Poulon chainsaw or a closet organizer.

Gifts for people you despise:

Let's face it. Your Christmas list includes people you wish would join a cloistered religious order or the Federal Witness Protection Program. Forget the fruitcakes for these folks. Instead consider this year's Tony Fitzpatrick commemorative Christmas plate.

Yes, the famed artist, radio personality and Bard of Villa Avenue has fired up the kiln and come out with a beautiful 8-inch diameter plate showing Santa having a tattoo removed while the leather-jacketed Donner and Blitzen look on.

But what if Tony is already out of these hot-selling plates? Then send people you despise an unassembled closet organizer or tickets to a do-it-yourself "Messiah."

No Foam Home or pecan logs on the perfect family trip

HEY, IT'S MEMORIAL DAY Weekend, which means summer is here, which means we'll probably have to take a family vacation. Aaaiiieee! Quick, Watson, the Thorazine.

Here's the thing about family vacations: Men never have a good time on them. Oh, I know most wives will disagree with this. Right now there are probably hundreds of women soaking in tubs of hot water spiked with baking soda, reading this column between Harlequin Romances, shaking their heads and clucking, "Not my Fred, he loved our last trip to Lookout Mountain."

Not true, lady. Fred lied to you. Once alone with close male friends, Fred confided, "Jeez, the kids were real jerks and my wife was on me the full time about my drinking and my dead-end job and now we're in hock another $500 to VISA."

You see, the problem with family vacations is that you have to spend time with your family. To make matters worse, you have to spend this time in places like DisneyWorld—"Hey, hon, let's cough up a couple of grand so we can stand in line for four days with the kids and have mannequins tell us about hydroponics."

Even more horrifying, you'll probably drive there and along the way eat in restaurants that sell pecan logs, elevating your cholesterol level while rubbing elbows with the flannel shirt crowd and people who have read *Mandingo*.

And then let's not forget those radical mood swings that women go through while traveling:

He: Wow! You really can see five states from up here. I hope they sell bumper stickers.

She: I've decided to paint the front hall taupe, get my legs waxed, put both kids in Montessori school, become a Mary Kay representative, run for the school board... .

An hour later: He: Wanna stop at the next Stuckey's and buy your mother one of those mercury-filled birds that drinks water from a glass?

She: Leave my mother out of this.

He: Hey, a Dansk Factory Outlet. Wanna stop and get a new pot?

She: Is sex all men ever think about?

It's a hopeless scenario that creates undo stress on all family men. Children complicate the situation even further:

Father: After we go to the water-ski show we'll hit Fort Dells and then the Foam Home.

Children: We want to go back to the motel and play Nintendo.

Father: Then we'll eat at Paul Bunyan's and take a duck trip, and I'll do my best to get you kids autographed pictures of Tommy Bartlett.

Children: We're missing "The Simpsons."

This is why New York City is the perfect place for a family vacation. There kids learn valuable lessons in life:

Father: See that guy over there?

Children: You mean the barefoot guy pushing the shopping cart full of aluminum cans?

Father: That's the one. He majored in cultural anthropology at the University of Illinois. Don't let that happen to you.

Children: We want to go back to the hotel room and play Nintendo.

Father: They stole it last night.

Women never get depressed in New York:

He: Let's take the kids to the Metropolitan Museum of Art this afternoon.

She: Go ahead. I'm getting my face peeled, and then I'll be at Bloomingdale's.

And men can earn the respect of frau und kinder:

Mother: Your father is socially inept.

Children: Then how come that woman in the bar downstairs keeps calling him "Big Boy"?

Sure beats hydroponics.

French get a bit Goofy as Disney slips 'em a Mickey

IT'S THE FRENCH AGAIN. AFTER years of filling our speech with *je ne sais quois, coups de grace* and *soups du jour,* they tell us we're fat and that the newly opened Euro Disney near Paris is corrupting their culture.

But the Disney people aren't in this for the money. They are on a mission to teach members of all races and ethnic groups to stand in line. So far, they have done a wonderful job here in America; just look at those unemployment lines on the nightly newscasts.

When you've got something good, why not export it? Isn't that what balance of trade is all about?

Unfortunately, the French don't like outsiders muscling in on their territory. And if France becomes Americanized, who in the future will buy all that Louis XIV furniture they have lying around? No wonder they are sensitive about their culture. They might have to resort to a national garage sale.

Anyway, their feelings run deep. Take a gander at some of the letters published in Paris dailies since the French Disneyland opened.

Cher Editor, Zut alors! Zee girlfriend of zee mouse shaves her legs!

Cher Editor, Zee fat Americaans zink zey will make us abandon our ways Français. We buy zere bleu pantaloons, zere rock musique, next we weel play baseball and let zee children into zee good restaurants. Do zey buy our Peugeots? Non! Disney ees too much.

Cher Editor, Ees Goofy a dog? Eef yes, zen why does not Pluto talk?

Cher Editor, How can zee nation where everybody owns a gun believe in zee talking mice? Zee characters Disney are as reediculous as zee fat Americaans. Are zese zee same people who give us Rambo, Shane and zee Bunch Wild? Eet cannot be.

Cher Editor, Moi does not like zee fast food of zee Americaans. Moi does like zere soft paper du toilet.

Cher Editor, Zee ice in zee soft drinks geeves moi zee freeze head.

Cher Editor, Zee changing-diaper table in zee men's toilet ees an insult to zee French male. We are a nation of Napoleons, DeGaulles and goose liver pate. Eef men Amerique wish to be servants domestique, let zem. Zee glory of France will not be spent wiping enfants' derrieres.

Cher Editor, Pourquoi does zee hair of zee Americaans smell like fruit and bushes? Eet make me sick.

Cher Editor, Zose crazy Americaans! Zey believe in flying elephants and mice zat wear clothes. Who helps zee mice get dressed?

Cher Editor, Zee waiters in zee restaurants Amerique are tres snobs. I order zee dog hot with Bordelaise sauce. Zey laugh at me with zere fat Americaan faces and pretend zey do not parlez Francais. I spit on zee duck called Donald.

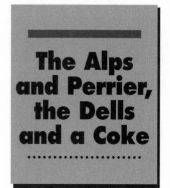

The Alps and Perrier, the Dells and a Coke

M Y 16-YEAR-OLD KID LEFT for Switzerland Sunday evening. Six years ago we exchanged sons with a French family through the local Back-to-Back program. We've been doing it on our own with the same French family ever since.

Every summer they leave Paris and spend a month hiking around the Alps. This is what happens in societies that don't have places like the Wisconsin Dells to blow off an occasional weekend.

Our son and their son have nothing in common. Before my kid's birth I dreamed of fathering the next Mozart, although a Gershwin or even a Marvin Hamlisch would have satisfied me. Instead I was given an offspring who tosses knuckleballs from April through August and runs around in knee sox bouncing soccer balls off his head for the remaining months of the year.

The French kid is a loner. The high point of his days here is riding my one-speed bicycle to Kohler's Trading Post to search for old radio and television vacuum tubes.

The last time he stayed with us he bought several hundred of them. "My collection," he said each night at the supper table as he showed us the day's acquisitions. But don't think the kid is one-dimensional; he also collects 78-rpm records and 8-track tape cartridges, which he enjoys disassembling on our kitchen counter top.

Anyway, preparations to get our kid on his way were more casual than for past trips. Midnight on Saturday he informed us that he was missing his favorite pair of walking shorts. "Why do you wait until midnight on Saturday to tell us something like that?" I said in my parent voice. He had no answer.

He slept until 11 a.m. Sunday. The favorite walking shorts reappeared and were folded and placed in his suitcase by his mother. "I can really pack," she said. It's true. In addition to two weeks of clothes including the favorite walking shorts and gifts for each member of the French family, she managed to stash a large box of Dots, and a half-pound of gummi Bears, four boxes of raisins, three V-8 drink boxes, a bag of Tato Skins, a jumbo Oh Henry bar and eight mini-Snickers.

"I wish I could take a couple of six-packs of Coke," the kid said. "They just have those little 8-ounce bottles, the kind you see in old movies."

"Drink Perrier," I told him.

He was to board the plane at 5 p.m. By 2 things were in high gear. His mother checked and rechecked the suitcase. "What do you want for your last meal?" I asked.

"Italian beef with no peppers, large order of fries and a small vanilla shake," he said. "And I want the same thing as soon as I get back."

"Isn't French food any good?" his ten-year-old brother asked.

"You've got to be 21 to enjoy it," he said.

About 4:30 we took him to O'Hare, checked him in at SwissAir and watched him depart.

"I'm going to take a couple of days off from work next week. Where do you want to go?" I asked my 10-year-old on the way back from the boarding gate.

"Dells," he said.

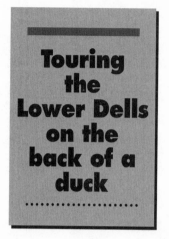

Touring the Lower Dells on the back of a duck

WISCONSIN DELLS, WIS. WE arrived Friday around noon and didn't have motel reservations, so we searched for a room. By 1 we found a place without a No Vacancy sign.

An old woman who had a thick accent that sounded Ukrainian told me the rooms went for $65 a night, but if I wanted the deluxe room with two king-sized beds, it would be another saw-buck. While she talked she chewed on a piece of coffee cake, and little bits of nuts and streusel fell from her mouth onto the registration desk.

I gave her a 50-dollar bill and a 20. She excused herself to get change from the owner.

A few minutes later a man chewing intently on a sandwich walked toward us across the parking lot. "What is this, a Polident commercial?" I said to the kid, who didn't laugh.

"She's old and don't remember the prices. It's $75 a night for the cheap room and $85 for the deluxe," the owner said.

Must have seen my Illinois plates, I thought, and told him 75 bucks was too steep. In the car I explained to the kid that the world is full of empty motel rooms and we'd find one soon. But he gave me that can't-we-do-stuff-like-normal-people look that my kids are always giving me.

We tried several more places before we found one that had a room available. It cost $75 plus tax and I could only get it for one night.

"How much was it?" the kid asked.

"Fifty," I said.

We played 18 holes of miniature golf and after lunch rode around the Lower Dells in an amphibious duck. The tour cost $15 for the two of us, but before we were released our tour guide revealed that he was putting himself through the University of Iowa's marketing program solely by selling postcards for $3 a package to duck passengers—not a bad marketing strategy in itself.

I gave him six bucks but took only one package. What I'll do with black-and-white photos of the WWII Guadalcanal duck maintenance base is beyond me.

Saturday we searched for another motel room. Over breakfast I read the following story in the Wisconsin State Journal:

> "Racine—A rural homeowner accused of murdering a fundraiser who knocked at his door was quoted Friday as saying he shot the stranger in the head accidentally, then put the victim's brains in a garbage disposal to conceal the evidence... ."

"This is why I feel safer in Chicago," I told the kid as I showed him the story.

We spent the afternoon on an upper-Dells boat trip, watching a dog jump from one elevated rock to another. Our guide sold us a four-color booklet of the upper Dells for $3, and, as the boat headed toward the dock, the pilot reran the same spiel we heard the day before from the duck driver—"We don't earn a salary but earn only the money that our passengers give us." He passed around an empty Lipton's Iced Tea canister with a slit cut in the top.

I finally understood why it's called the Badger State.

This is the way things used to be, before the Interstate

LYNDON STATION, WIS. EVERY five or six hours in the Dells I'd grow tired of go-carts and miniature golf and tell the kid that I was getting claustrophobic. We'd head out to the country for an hour to catch our breath. It was on Friday afternoon that I found it.

About 8 miles northwest of the Dells on Route 12 a small town appears without the usual warnings of strip centers and convenience food stores. The speed limit drops from 65 to 35, the road smoothes out a bit, and you're on the main drag of Lyndon Station, Wisconsin.

In the middle of town where Route 12 intersects County HH is the Lyndo Inn. We happened on it by chance. "Why do you always find places like this?" the kid asked as we sat at a window table.

It was mid afternoon. An old man at the counter smoked cigarettes, and little circles of smoke trailed upward toward the tin ceiling. "I bet if we came back tomorrow, he'd still be here," the kid said.

Men parked their trucks outside and came in for coffee or left messages for one another with the waitress. They would then be on their way—clearly not the cellular phone crowd. Four men wearing belts and suspenders sat in a corner booth and talked passionately about engines and winches.

"This is the way things used to be," I told the kid. "Before interstates you'd drive through small towns, and if you wanted something to eat, you stopped in places like this."

I was sounding preachy. On an enclosed porch near the dining room the Lyndo Inn acknowledged the last decade of the 20th century with a couple of video games. I gave the kid three quarters.

Daily specials were posted on huge Blatz Beer signs that hung above the counter. "You serve Blatz?" I asked the waitress.

"Naw," she said. "We just use the signs." The kid ordered a cheeseburger with fries and I had the meatloaf and mashed pota-toes. The bill with a couple of Cokes was $6.88.

"How late you open?" I asked the owner, a thin, mustached man who wore a copper bracelet.

"I don't turn the lights out until 11 every night," he said. We came back in the morning for breakfast. The same old guy smoked at the counter. "I could be happy here," I told the kid. "I could sit here for a year and write a novel." I sounded preachy again and gave him a couple of quarters for the video games.

Whole families came and went that morning, and not just par-ents and kids: aunts, uncles and grandparents sat together at long tables.

"They call that tall guy 'Shorty,'" the kid observed. I liked it that he noticed such things.

The waitress, a high school girl who looked like Molly Ringwald, spilled milk twice and laughed each time. We went back to the Dells to drive go-karts and played more miniature golf on courses designed by Liberace.

At 11 that night we drove by the Lyndo Inn again. The lights were still on.

An $85 brunch can be a bargain

IT'S ALMOST EASTER, A MAJOR Christian holiday and an excuse for a family of four to blow 85 bucks on eggs Benedict. And that's served cafeteria-style.

Face it, brunch is a bizarre Western concept. According to the dictionary, the word came into common usage in 1896.

Even though brunches pre-date me, as a kid I never attended one; my German grandmother wouldn't allow it. "If you want to stand in line for food, join the army," she said.

I never argued with her. This was the same woman who threw her slippers at the television whenever Mayor Daley or Charles DeGaulle appeared on the screen. My early restaurant experiences were confined to Mader's in Milwaukee or Phil Schmidt's in Indiana. If either served brunch, I never was aware of it.

Anyway, I don't know who in the 1890s decided to put breakfast and lunch together, but it was probably the English. Making one English meal from two means there's one fewer to suffer through.

Americans now fully embrace brunching, and the Easter brunch has become as traditional as Christmas dinner or the Weberizing of cow on the Fourth of July.

Brunches are ideal for kids. The national adolescent attention span, which for years hovered around 30 minutes—the same time occupied by most TV sitcoms—is now 3 minutes 30 seconds, thanks to rock videos.

This means members of the MTV generation need 16.2 new activities introduced every hour or they become whining ninnies or give you the old adolescent sulk routine.

Consider the following: a family eating in a restaurant circa 1959.

Adolescent: Dad, we've been here almost an hour. I'm bored. Can we go? We're missing "Spin and Marty."

Dad: Shut up. Keep your elbows off the table and eat like a gentleman. We'll leave when your mother and I are ready.

Consider the same scene in the '90s.

Adolescent: Dad, I broke the hand dryer in the washroom because there is nothing to do. We've been here almost seven minutes.

Dad: Damn! And this place doesn't even have a video arcade. You and your brother can use the car phone to call 900 numbers, and I'll tell the waitstaff to hurry.

Of course, a sticky situation such as the above can be easily avoided by taking the kids to brunch.

Adolescent: Dad, if I don't have something to do soon, I'll drive you and mom nuts by talking while chewing on ice cubes.

Dad: No thanks. Jonathan Demme's Oscar acceptance was bad enough. Grab a couple plates of stuffed salmon en croute and empty them into the plastic bag in your mother's purse.

Adolescent: What about beef Wellington?

Dad: Take some of that too. This way we can pork out at home and watch "In Living Color" or "Nova."

The problem with kids and brunches is that kids only appreciate cuisine that comes enclosed in Styrofoam. They'd be happier at McDonald's or anywhere else they could make moaning whale sounds by rubbing a plastic straw through the opening of a soft-drink lid.

Whale sounds or no, eating together is part of the socialization process. If you don't take kids out to restaurants once in a while, they might become socially maladjusted adults or accountants. Eighty-five bucks for four orders of eggs Benedict every Easter is worth it.

Especially if you throw in a hand dryer.

■

Career options from gambling on stocks to "Something Crazy"

IT WAS ONE OF THOSE THINGS parents are supposed to do with their kids. Over Christmas vacation we took both boys to the Chicago Board of Options Exchange.

The idea was that we'd stand in the gallery overlooking the trading floor and watch fortunes being made. Thirty years hence, when our kids would be interviewed by Forbes, they'd look back and say, "We owe all our success to our parents who took an entire day to show us the ins and outs of the world's financial markets."

The Exchange's movers and shakers were elsewhere. A few bored traders batted crumpled paper balls with rolled up Wall Street Journals. No fortunes were being made on the last trading day of 1989.

We watched a video tape that explained what an option is and why investors buy them. Various officers of the exchange explained the importance of trading to the general health and well-being of the American public.

"You ever buy options?" the kid asked.

"Until six months ago, I didn't have a savings account," I said. "And after seeing these guys play baseball, my advice to you is the same advice my grandfather gave me: Buy a two-flat and live in the basement."

A light rain fell as we walked West on Van Buren Street toward the car. "This is my favorite part of the Loop," I said. "The conservatory I went to is only a couple of blocks east of here." Both kids made a face.

I talked to the parking lot attendant, a big Latvian guy in his 60s from Riga.

"North side or south side of Riga?" I asked. He didn't get it, but he did tell my wife her winter coat made her look like a Russian soldier.

I explained to the kids how I had worked for several years as a parking lot attendant and how we made coffee money by selling the same parking space twice using only one register receipt. They made that face again and so did Comrade Mom.

Having seen enough of the twentieth century, we waited in line for the Field Museum's Egyptian exhibit. One of the plaques explained that the ancients weren't as obsessed with death as we think. It's just that our only glimpses of their culture are through their burial artifacts. I worried that future civilizations might view ours through "Cosby Show" reruns:

"The ancients loved to wear bright, multi-colored sweaters. Although parents always had successful careers, the female spent the greater part of her day sharing wisdom and nurturing her off-spring while the male parent made silly faces."

Lake Shore Drive was bumper-to-bumper as we headed toward Evanston. The final stop for culture day was Northwestern University. We hoped that after seeing the campus, both kids would develop perfect table manners, sell their Nintendo games and speak French at dinner.

They threw snowballs as my wife delivered a lecture on her alma mater's architecture but stopped as she spoke of the student strike during the Vietnam War and how college kids blocked Sheridan Road to protest Nixon's policies.

"What do you think I should do for a living?" my fifteen-year-old asked later that night.

"You're talking to a guy who got his first real job when he was forty-three," I said. "I'm not the one to give career advice."

"Yeah," he said. "But what would you like to see me do?"

"Something crazy," I told him.

LOCAL COLOR

Beer and urban renewal

IT'S THOSE ELMHURST CITY planners again. Every few months they hatch another scheme to raise the collective blood pressure of local taxpayers.

Before city planners arrived, downtown Elmhurst wasn't much to look at. Throw in a grain and feed store, a Massey-Ferguson dealer and a few rustics with hairy ears and it could have passed for an Iowa farm town. But who wants to pay real estate taxes that cause nosebleeds and live in an Iowa farm town?

We needed a downtown that would rival Hinsdale's and Glen Ellyn's—"Elmhurst city planners, we want to boutique with the best of 'em."

Besides having a bad self-image, our downtown's economic whoozitz was shrinking. We had to do something to stop the inmates from shopping in Oak Brook. So we built a police station without a front door and a neo-Lego apartment building.

Now comes the hard part. Moving city offices around is one thing, but retail redevelopment is another. Besides occupying new storefronts, retailers have to turn a profit.

This is why I will attend the next Elmhurst City Council meeting and urge council members to terminate the contracts of all professional planners now used by the city so they may find honest employment as hod carriers and carny workers.

Once the professional guys are gone, I want local movers and shakers to adopt my simple plan.

■

Ask any shopping center developer what the most important component of a profitable operation is and he or she will reply, "an anchor store."

With an anchor store you have stability, bliss and something to build around. Without one you'll wind up with a glorified strip mall full of kids wearing black T-shirts and riding 20-inch bikes.

This is why I am suggesting the city give the old Walgreen's building (Elm Square Building) to the Baderbrau Brewery with the stipulation that the brewery move all production there. Beer is our best anchor.

But we wouldn't leave the building the way it is. We'd retro-fit it with exterior transparent pipe so passers-by could watch the ebb and flow of the brewing process. It would look like France's Georges Pompidou Center but instead of heating ducts and electrical conduit on the outside, we'd have beer pipelines. Then we'd change the city motto from "Motor in Horto" (plenty of free parking) to "Beer is Good" (beer is good).

Elmhurst would be the only Chicago suburb with a brewery at its heart. No more looking down at the floor at Hinsdale cocktail parties when the hostess raves about seeing depressing subtitled movies at the local cinema. We won't need Bergman films in downtown Elmhurst because we'll have a brewery.

Those uppity Evanston people may brag about having Northwestern University and the lakefront, but Evanston does not now and never will have a brewery. Neither will Winnetka, Oak Park or Barrington—you name the place, it doesn't and never will have one.

We have a brewery in town already, but it's tucked away in an industrial park as if it's a hardware supply company. It belongs downtown.

Move it and we could have a summer beer garden and have an accordion player who knows all the choruses to "Schnitzelbank." Busses from Lexington Square could drop off seniors who want to grab a couple of short cold ones on summer afternoons. Commuters could stop on their way home and bend their elbows for a while.

"Beer is Good."

Night out in DuPage

CHICAGO MAGAZINE'S AUGUST issue devotes several pages to questions and answers on where to go for a night out. Oddly enough, those smarmy Chicago staffers did not recommend a single restaurant, theater or bowling alley in DuPage County; it's as if they don't recognize our existence.

Everybody can't blow 400 big ones on a frame two-flat in Wrigleyville, another 250 big ones to rehab it and still have money left over for a Porsche and lambada lessons. Hey, maybe we're not chic or trendy, but we of DuPage like to get out once in a while, too.

Anyway, I thought this would be a good time to answer the most frequently asked questions about a night on the town in DuPage.

Where's a good place to eat after midnight on a Sunday night? This is tough. Aside from places occupied by overweight cigarette smokers and Grateful Dead roadies, there isn't much open in DuPage that late on a Sunday night.

We recommend you buy a couple of pieces of fruit and a bottle of wine from the Cub Foods on Roosevelt Road in Lombard (it's open 24 hours a day!) and then have a romantic picnic on the Illinois Prarie Path. Watch out for geezers wearing trench coats and teen-agers with 666 tattooed on their foreheads.

Where's a place to get good Chinese food? DuPage has a number of wonderful Chinese restaurants. My favorite is China Chef in Westmont. Oddly enough, Westmont is a Democratic stronghold in Republican DuPage. I sometimes take my kids there just to show them what Democrats look like.

Are there any special places where my wife and I can go to explore the realm of the senses together? You bet. There's the legendary Sybaris Motel on Ogden Avenue in Downers Grove. Here couples can frolic on waterbeds under mirrored ceilings, watch X-rated videos together and experiment with a Taiwan basket (don't ask). Of course, if you really want a place that sets the mood with that special someone, we suggest Villa Park's Brer Rabbit Motel on North Avenue just west of Route 83. Be sure to tip the concierge.

We have three kids younger than six. Are there any good restaurants that don't discriminate against a family with toddlers? There probably are, but a night out with kids is not a night out. Why drop sixty to a hundred bucks to watch somebody chew with his mouth open? Your best bet is to leave the kids overnight with your in-laws and you and your spouse have a real night out—Taiwan basket and all.

What if I don't have in-laws? Normally, I don't make offers like this, but if you and yours really need a night out alone, drop your kids off at my house and pick them up the following morning. Be sure to bring Velcro restraining straps, a set of jumper cables and a tape of at least one episode of "Twin Peaks."

Are there any intimate jazz clubs like Chicago's ever-crowded Gold Star Sardine Bar in DuPage County? Regrettably, no. But all is not lost. If you want to experience much the same ambience as the Gold Star, we suggest you drop in at your local Blockbuster Video and rent "Jazz on a Summer's Day" and "Chet Baker: Let's Get Lost." Then invite numerous friends to your hall closet to watch them.

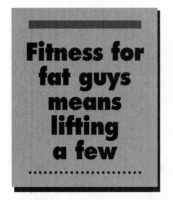

Fitness for fat guys means lifting a few

I T'S HARD ENOUGH TO CATCH A little sleep around my house; I have two kids who incessantly listen to rap music while dribbling a soccer ball from room to room. But on Thanksgiving morning it became even more impossible.

I was awakened by the padding of a thousand runners. The starting line for the annual Turkey Trot, an event for athletic anorexics was only two blocks away.

Once started, joggers coursed down our street, some running through my side yard and across the lawn. "Excuse us," one said as he leaped over an evergreen. "Jeez, I wish I had a couple of land mines," I said to a neighbor who assumed I was joking.

What bothered me was not the runners' disgustingly wholesome attitudes, but that they are thin and I am not. Occasionally, I could see a wide body in the gaggle of greyhounds. For the most part, though, the runners looked as if they took those Jane Fonda exercise tapes too seriously.

I felt lonely and left out as I watched them. "My cholesterol is under 200, what's yours?" a participant yelled to me as he trotted by. I've had enough of this second-class citizenship. Thus, I have decided to sponsor a fitness event for fat guys. Probably the only one of its kind, we want to show the world that fitness belongs to everyone, not just those who are in shape.

It will take place at 11 a.m. New Year's Day, 1991. We will gather at my house, only two blocks from the starting line of the Thanksgiving Day debacle, do some stretching exercises and eat a cold pizza from the party the night before.

At the sound of the starting gun we will walk 1,020 steps to a nearby convenience food store, where we can catch our collective breath and buy a paper before completing the last leg, another 433 steps, to a popular Elmhurst bar. There we'll lift a few and call spouses for rides back to the starting line. In case of inclement weather we'll cancel everything or drive the entire course.

Just like those events for skinny people, the Loose Change "Fat Guys Only Fitness Walk" will give each participant a commemorative T-shirt. The only requirement is that applicants tip the old Toledo at more than 200 pounds and have a waist measurement greater than their inseam.

Of course, some thin guys will try to crash the party, but I will personally administer a little test that I have devised: Each entrant will be asked to tie his shoes while carrying on a conversation. If he can talk while bent over, he's an obvious imposter and won't get a free T-shirt.

If you are interested, fill out the form below and send it back to me pronto. We'll be in touch and please, nobody wear those Spandex outfits.

The Beef Shift accepts 'big' fitness challenges

THE IDEA IS A SIMPLE ONE: A fitness event for fat guys. My plan is to get together on New Year's Day with a bunch of people who would like to kick Richard Simmons in the sweetbreads. We'll have a starting line, just like runners do, and at the sound of the starter's gun we will walk en masse to a nearby bar, where we will lift a few and pass out the commemorative T-shirts before going to dinner at the in-laws'. It will be an anti-90s statement.

A number of people—both men and women—have signed up. But the most interesting correspondence comes from Robert "R.C." Chalupa of the Roselle Police Association.

Dear Jack:

Your column on the Loose Change Fat Guys Only Fitness Walk immediately brought to mind a whole bunch of guys who would love to take part in this historic event. My entire shift, commonly called "The Beef Shift," by some act of nature is off on New Year's Day!

Following is a list of our applicants for the event. All are members of the Roselle Police Department except one; he will be our designated driver. And all wear a 2XL T—shirt: Patrick "Demps" Dempsey, George "Upsidedown" Kasnick, Bob "Big Bob" Mitchell, Lenny "Where's Lunch?" Notz, Russell "Torpedo" Stokes and Edward "Father" Windle.

I could not present you with a more qualified bunch of guys. I assume you will be getting back to us as to the starting point. Special training for such an event is unnecessary because we train on a daily basis.

Sincerely,

Robert Chalupa

There you have it—cops who actually look like cops. In

recent years there has been an effort by police departments to recruit officers who look as if they had stepped out of a Guess Jean commercial. It's wonderful that some of these guys can compete in a triathalon and have low cholesterol levels, but if your neighborhood is being invaded by teen-age street gangs, do you really want Charlie Sheen and Sean Penn to show up in police uniforms? No thanks, give me the Roselle Beef Shift.

Anyway, the Fat Guys Only Fitness Walk is scheduled for 11 a.m. on New Year's Day.

Don't forget to bring chafing powder.

The sound of fat guys marching

O K FAT GUYS, FALL IN BEHIND me in a column of fours; road guards out at the intersections. Forward ho! Liiift, Riiight, Liiift, Riiight. All right gentlemen, sound off. *We don't care 'bout ca-lo-ries, 'Cause we eat food as we please...*

This Fat Guy's Fitness Event started off simply enough. I watched a bunch of Spandex-wearing ninnies run by my house on Thanksgiving Day and thought there should be something like that for fat guys. A neighbor and I came up with the idea of inviting portly types over on New Year's Day to walk en masse to a local bar and lift a few. It would be the anti-fitness statement of the '90s. I wrote a column about it and a bunch of people jumped on the bandwagon, including one entire shift of the Roselle Police Department.

A fellow scribe at this newspaper suggested that a more appropriate route would be to start at the Entenmann's Bakery on North Avenue in Northlake and end at the Baderbrau Brewery in Elmhurst. That will be the route. I checked it out, and the total distance is only nine-tenths of a mile. But I caution those of you who are interested, the first twenty feet are uphill—please don't get a nosebleed. We'll meet at 11 a.m. on New Year's Day at Entenmann's, knock off several dozen sweet rolls and then head for the Baderbrau Brewery, where Ken Pavichevich will hand out glasses of his finest to replenish the nutrients lost on the grueling .9-mile course.

If you are fat and feel like being in your own Rose Bowl Parade, show up for this milestone in the history of American obesity. Even if you're not fat, come anyway and cheer for your favorite wide body. Lift, riiight, lift, riiight...

Gentlemen, it's time to honor the memory of great fat people, both living and dead: Orson Welles, Jackie Gleason, Williard Scott, W.C. Fields, Edwin Meese, William Howard Taft. And let's not forget the ladies: Roseanne Barr, Jessye Norman, Kate Smith. All great people of immodest girth who lived productive lives without ever wearing Spandex or going on a liquid protein diet. Sound off, gentlemen.

Oprah's diet made her small,
But she started eatin' and regained it all.

Anyway, there seems to be a lot of interested fat guys out there. A number of them signed up for the event after reading Loose Change. Then I was interviewed by WLUP radio and Copley News Service. The Sun-Times ran a short piece about it—get this, in the sports section—and Crain's Chicago Business called it "The biggest race of the year."

In the last few days, a number of half-looped overweights at office Christmas parties called me about signing up and bringing along extra-large friends. I must have talked to most of the porkers in North America.

Originally I had stipulated that only those 200 pounds or heavier with waist measurements larger than their inseams could participate. A number of people in the 190 range asked if they could carry a couple of bricks in their pockets. That's unnecessary. If you're even near 200, that's close enough for us. And if you're over 200 pounds and because of some genetic flaw have an inseam greater than your waist, wear Bermuda shorts. See you there.

Liiift, Riiight, Liiift, Riiight. (I love writing that.)

Municipal juice, Walden Pond

A YEAR AGO THE CITY OF Elmhurst sent me a renewal notice for my pickup truck's vehicle sticker. Usually I wait until six months past the deadline, then pay an extra couple of bucks in penalties. But this time I decided to pass on the whole thing. For some reason it bothered me that I was supposed to shell out $30 for the privilege of driving around Elmhurst in a Third World vehicle with a leaking radiator while my wife paid a paltry $12 for the use of the same streets but in a Toyota with a sun roof. Life is not fair, nor is marriage.

"You know you'll get one sooner or later, so why don't you do it now, before you have a pile of tickets to pay?" she warned.

"It's the principle," I said. "Whatever happened to all that stuff we talked about in the sixties? Thoreau, civil disobedience, Lucite salad bowls...." She was unimpressed.

Just as dependable as nature, the Elmhurst Police Department ticketed my vehicle. And just as dependable as nature, the tickets were tossed under the seat. I grew a beard and read *Walden.*

If a vehicle sticker fine is left unpaid for five days, a notice is mailed to the offender that the penalty has doubled, sort of a municipal juice loan.

Little stuff like that doesn't bother civil libertarians, though; I put the notices on top of the refrigerator with the unpaid utility bills. "Why don't you just get a sticker," a female officer asked as she wrote me still another one. "It would be cheaper than paying for all these tickets."

I didn't answer. How can you explain Thoreau to Dirty Harriet? Besides, I wasn't going to pay for them. I planned to go to court and testify on my own behalf. They'd toss me in the cooler. Soviet Jews would go on hunger strikes. The whole thing would be an embarrassment to the U.S. of A. Eventually, a higher court would reverse the decision, and Morton Downey would have me on his program.

Months went by. More notices arrived and were deposited on top of the refrigerator. A scofflaw friend of mine had the Denver Boot placed on his car. I began riding a bicycle. Ghandi probably went through the same stuff. Just before Christmas things came to a head.

"The cops are here looking for you," my wife informed.

"They use tear gas or Miranda-ize the kids?"

"No, but they want to see you down at the station right away." I thought about grabbing some blankets and hiding out on the Prairie Path until the whole thing blew over, but that's not what civil disobedience is all about.

"Sign these," the cop said as he handed me a fistful of papers. I had known his wife from years before.

"How's your wife?" I asked, hoping he'd not try to beat a confession out of me.

"We're divorced."

"What do I do next?"

"Go across the street and pay them $240."

"What if I want to go to court?"

"What are ya gonna do, plead insanity?"

I folded. Morton Downey would have to wait, but on the other hand, Soviet Jews could keep eating.

"What happened to Thoreau?" my wife asked after I confessed to shelling out 240 simoleons.

"He's on top of the refrigerator."

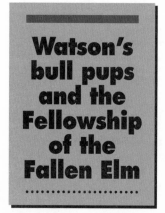

Watson's bull pups and the Fellowship of the Fallen Elm

ELMHURST IS A NORMAL TOWN. It has a library, hospital, college and the standard roster of service clubs: Lions, Kiwanis and Rotary. It also has a number of social organizations: a bicycle club, a German choir, numerous church affiliated groups, a gardening club, a photography club—you name it, Elmhurst has it. Except for a hospital and college, most suburbs have these things.

But Elmhurst is unique in that it has Watson's Bull Pups and the Fellowship of the Fallen Elm—two Sherlock Holmes Clubs. Originally there was only Watson's Bull Pups. It met monthly, which became every six weeks, then every couple of months.

Prior to the September meeting, Bull Puppies last saw one another three years ago. That was fine for most Bull Pups. Arthur Conan Doyle is dead. There aren't going to be any new stories to discuss, so what's the rush? But every organization has true believers and those who are just along for the ride. The true believer Bull Puppies felt that no meeting for three years signaled the demise of the club, and that it was time to start another one. Thus, the Fellowship of the Fallen Elm. Remaining Bull Puppies denied their demise.

"We were just taking a nap," they said, and immediately scheduled a September get-together—six middle-aged guys, eight bottles of wine, forty-eight bottles of beer and three cheese balls.

I have never missed a Bull Pups' meeting. Perfect attendance is no great accomplishment, especially when three years elapse between meetings. But it is a great accomplishment considering I have never completely read a Sherlock Holmes story. I like the plots but can't stand the writing. Consider a sentence from "The Adventure of Wisteria Lodge," Bull Puppies' assigned reading for the soon-to-be-postponed October meeting. "A cold and melancholy walk of a couple of miles brought us to a high wooden gate, which opened into a gloomy avenue of chestnuts."

Translation: The walk depressed us.

Thank God for VCRs. Like all English writers, Arthur Conan Doyle floats his stories on a sea of modifiers. Take out the adjectives and adverbs, toss in some sex and you've got a Victorian Mickey Spillane. For me it wouldn't matter, though; I don't read Mickey Spillane either.

I have considered starting a third Elmhurst Sherlock Holmes club for non-readers like me. Instead of monthly meetings, I would offer club members my own rewrites of classic Holmes stories delivered through the mail:

> "The Adventure of Wisteria Lodge." *Scott Eccles was light in the loafers and spent too much time alone. Holmes took his case, but Holmes takes most cases—otherwise he'd spend his days playing the violin; Heifetz he's not...*

But a third club for people like me is unnecessary. Bull Puppies embrace everyone, even non-readers. At our September meeting/three year reunion we hardly mentioned Holmes, Watson, Doyle or modifiers. Instead we had a lengthy discussion on what every middle-aged man fears the most: not death, impeded sexual performance or a big stomach—but waking up in the hospital just in time for a catheter insertion. Everybody told his favorite catheter story. I got so sick I couldn't finish the cheese balls.

It was good to see these guys again.

New beaten paths beckon: Why ask why? Just do it.

"DAY TRIPS," MY EDITOR said. "Starting next week our Family Living section is doing a series on day trips."

Not a bad idea, I thought. I take day trips whenever possible, and I wouldn't mind writing about a few of my favorites. "We'll be rich," I said to the wife. "Call the dealership and schedule both cars for oil changes."

"Does that include filters too?" she asked.

"Give 'em the works," I said. "Nothing's too good for my Festiva."

It was then I realized these day trips for the Family Living section are supposed to include kids, a significant other, a minivan, at least one golden retriever—maybe even a canoe, Gore-Tex clothing and those stupid fanny packs. "Forget the oil changes," I said. "I'll get a haircut instead."

Taking along the people you live with defeats the purpose of a day trip. Isn't the idea to get away from familiar surroundings, family members and overdraft notices to do something physically and mentally invigorating?

To do this, you've got to head out alone. So, lace up your hiking boots, grab an L.L. Bean catalog or a copy of Thoreau's *Walden* and a four-wheel-drive vehicle with a gun rack. Over the next several weeks "Loose Change" will offer its own day-tripping series for loners, practitioners of alternative lifestyles, and unemployed, middle-age people who need a break from their in-laws.

Without further ado, here's Loose Change Day Trip No. 1— Destination: The Fire Bell Pub, 172 Addison Ave., Elmhurst, Ill.

• How to get there: Drive four-wheel-drive vehicle to 172 Addison Ave., Elmhurst, Ill. Park in back.

• What to wear: Shirt, pants and shoes. No Lycra outfits, please.

• What to bring: $10.

- What not to bring: Copies of Proust's *Remembrance of Things Past,* Montessori teaching certificate, Filofax notebook.
- Good points: Judy, the daytime bartender. All-you-can-eat fish fry every Friday. Old Style is only $1 a glass. Exotic bar snacks include beef jerky and popcorn. Customers don't bring their dogs. Electronic and old-fashioned dart games available. Side room ideal for business meetings and after-funeral luncheons. 1950s decor throughout. Just-planted flowers (impatiens) in front of building. Nearby food store sells breath mints. Mitsubishi 45-inch television.
- Bad Points: Mitsubishi 45-inch television. Judy, the daytime bartender, sometimes chews ice. Parking lot in rear not suitable for rollerblading. Elmhurst College faculty members sometimes frequent the place and discuss Southern writers. Very high urinals.
- Trivia: The bar is exactly 44 feet long. The one remaining barstool with a back is called "The Cadillac" by regular customers. The Fire Bell first opened in 1954. When forced to work past 5 p.m., Judy, now in her 17th year of bartending and psychodrama, turns radio to U.S. 99.
- Most unusual employee practice: During peak periods Judy sometimes saves places for regular customers by putting phoney drinks on bar.
- Most unusual occurrence in recent memory: After removing money from sock to pay bar tab, a customer talked to himself at length, then hit his order of fried fish with his shoe.

Evolution linked to the water

THE CHANGE IN DUPAGE WAS so gradual that it wasn't noticed until years later by historians.

The last decade of the 20th century came and went with most residents feeling things were much the same as they had been. But that's the way sweeping changes take place.

In the mid-1990s people noticed the newsstand on the corner of North Avenue and Route 83, but it drew little comment. Neither did the construction of sidewalks in Oak Brook. By the end of the decade several Oak Brook residents not clothed in Spandex were seen walking.

A few years later, Naperville was commended for building an el. Other DuPage communities rushed to imitate. "Mass transit reduces traffic congestion and air pollution," several village managers said as they applied for federal subsidies.

Still, nobody saw the bigger picture. A few eyebrows were raised when March 17 became a county holiday. A few more were raised when Lisle celebrated Gay Pride Day with a parade down Ogden Ave.

By the year 2000, all garbage trucks operating in DuPage had five-man crews. New subdivisions in Naperville and Bartlett had alleys. And local precinct captains awarded voters 55-gallon garbage cans for their support.

Neighborhood bars became common in Wheaton. While vacationing at a Caribbean singles resort in 2005, a young man met a young woman. "I'm from DuPage!" the woman informed him.

"North or South Side?" The man asked with some suspicion. After discovering they were from opposite ends of the county, they went their separate ways. She pursued a landscape artist from Omaha; he took up with an actuary from the Twin Cities.

In 2010, remembered by most as the year of the first Venetian Night on Salt Creek, Glen Ellyn residents changed the name of their village to Beverly. The local Harold Washington Party was instrumental in collecting signatures for the referendum.

The Elmhurst Symphony became the world's loudest orchestra. Several members of the Chicago Symphony's brass section were hospitalized for depression.

DuPage adopted a uniform street-numbering system. "What hunnert west is Schmale?" cabbies asked fares.

Hinsdale eventually changed its name to Sauganash. Residents then left their cars on the street overnight.

A county ordinance that was passed at the turn of the 21st century required all new construction at the College of DuPage to have turrets and gargoyles.

In 2008 a COD faculty member won the Nobel Peace Prize for his work on demand-side economics. He promptly shaved his head and became a presidential advisor.

County residents often took out-of-town guests for Wendella boat rides on Herrick's Lake.

Entourages from DuPage-area school districts begged for funds in Springfield. "The place is a financial sinkhole," Downstate politicians said of DuPage.

Eric Zorn's column replaced Royko's on page 3 in the Trib's DuPage editions. At a Democratic fund-raiser in 2024, the DuPage County Board chairman finished his speech with the words, "We have a wunnerful county full of wunnerful people."

He then toasted those present with a glass of Chicago water.

A
marching
band
for
serious
musicians
only

IT WAS ANOTHER MEMORIAL DAY parade. A few floats went by. Cub Scout packs and Brownies walked with their leaders. The local junior high and high school band marched too.

The Fourth of July won't be much different. But there will be more antique cars, maybe a couple of drum and bugle corps, and a Shriner motorcycle troop.

I marched in my share of parades. In high school I played trombone in a band that averaged a parade a week in good weather.

In college I made a few extra bucks by playing with Italian feast bands. We were paid ten bucks a day to march around Italian neighborhoods behind a statue of a saint while playing band arrangements of Italian opera favorites. Then there were my four years as a Navy bandsman. Every Fourth of July we marched in three parades and played a concert of patriotic favorites before the fireworks show. If you hand me a trombone in the middle of the night, I can still knock off "Anchors Aweigh," "Stars and Stripes Forever" and "The Thunderer."

But I digress. Yesterday, as I watched a color guard march to a recording of Sousa's "High School Cadets," which was broadcast from roof-mounted loudspeakers on a trailing minivan, I realized that the parades of today are hollow shells of those of years past.

There were once adult marching bands. American Legion posts, factories and civic organizations all sponsored them. In every parade there was at least one killer band from a Legion post in Lemont or South Milwaukee or some other place that nobody thought about for the rest of the year. The band was full of dentists who played E-flat peck horns and flute-playing lawyers. As the band passed, bystanders would elbow one another. "Did you hear that?" they'd say.

Kids from high school bands would stand in open-mouthed

awe as one of these killer bands struck up Sousa's "Bullets and Bayonets" or Josef Wagner's "Under the Double Eagle."

But that was then and this is now. Today we march to taped music. I guess that's progress.

But what is so good about progress? Recorded parade music doesn't give you goosebumps, nor does it make the hair on the back of your neck stand up. So what's the point of having it?

This is why I've decided to form the Loose Change Real Marching Band. Real bands play real marches—there will be no pop tunes in my band. If you once played an instrument or still do and want to attempt some real march music, drop me a line care of this paper and you'll be a charter member of The Loose Change Real Marching Band.

Because it's my band, it will play my favorites, starting with C.D. Pares' "The Chicago Tribune," which is twice as good as Sousa's "The Washington Post."

But we can't neglect the March King; purists become hysterical. So we'll play that campy little Sousa favorite, "Nobles of the Mystic Shrine."

In front of the reviewing stand we'll stand in place for a screamer, something really hard. I know you're thinking "Thunder and Blazes," but no thanks, everybody plays "Thunder and Blazes." We'll perform either "The Battle of Shiloh" or "The Storming of El Caney," two of the toughest marches ever written.

We've got a little more than a month before the Fourth of July parade and I want to hit the street with 72 people who can play their you-know-whats off. This isn't a social event. Only serious musicians wishing to recapture part of their youth and America's musical heritage need apply.

There will be free beer afterward.

Not a band but a whumper

I NEVER SAW HIM BEFORE. "YOU'RE really going to do it?" he asked.

"Huh?" I said.

"You know," he grinned. "The marching band." He was the 12th person to ask that day.

The previous week, while seeing a color guard march to recorded music in the Memorial Day parade, I came up with the idea of starting a marching band.

The idea is not unique. At one time every American Legion post, factory, civic organization and small Midwestern town of more that 60 people had one. But that was before cable, VCRs and Sony Walkmans.

These bands of yesterday were not student groups. Before professional sports became a mainline religion in this country, adults often did things that didn't involve projection TV or home entertainment systems. Community bands were popular.

All I want to do is recapture our lost greatness by finding 60 or 70 people who play a musical instrument well enough to walk down the street while performing three standard marches. It's not a big deal. I just want to march in the Elmhurst Fourth of July parade with a great-sounding band that plays three classics from the American band repertoire. Immediately afterward the Loose Change Marching Band will disband forever. Eight or 10 blocks and it fades into history.

You'd think I was attempting something hard, like understanding the property tax multiplier. People have asked a million questions. Here's a few:

Q. When do we rehearse?

A. One hour before the parade starts. We'll muster at the Fire Bell Pub on the morning of July 4 and take it from there.

Q. What if it rains?

A. The Fire Bell is indoors.

Q. What about music?

A. If you send me your address, I'll send you copies of your parts ahead of time. Otherwise you'll have to sight-read.

Q. What to wear?

A. Black slacks, white shirts or blouses and black shoes.

Q. How do you hope to attract enough good musicians to pull this off?

A. I'm buying a barrel of beer for the post-parade debriefing session.

Q. What marches will we play?

A. Definitely "National Emblem" because the trombone part to the trio goes "Whump, Whump, Whump, Whump." It's my favorite. Other than that, I'm open to suggestions.

Q. Wouldn't you like this to become a year-round activity so young students could be recruited into the band and have a place to use their God-given talents?

A. Nope.

Q. Have you obtained permission from the City of Elmhurst to march in this parade?

A. Must I do everything? Somebody take care of this little stuff; I've got to figure out a way to pay for the beer.

Q. Aside from our instruments, what else will we need?

A. Lyres, and if you don't know what a lyre is, I don't want you in my band.

Q. If this band is successful, is there a chance we might some-day march in other parades?

A. Nope.

Q. What is your experience in playing marches?

A. Four years of high school halftime shows and weekly parades; numerous appearances with Italian feast bands, which entailed walking through Italian neighborhoods while playing "The Italian Rifleman" in celebration of various saints' feast days; four years of daily parades while a Navy musician; and a year of playing the trombone on WGN's "Bozo's Circus."

Q. While you were on Bozo, did anyone make it to bucket no. 6 in the Grand Prize Game?

A. Nope.

Q. What is the real reason you're forming your own marching band?

A. I just want to hear six trombones play "Whump, Whump, Whump, Whump" again.

That was no bass drum; my heart was pounding

I WAS GETTING CALLS RIGHT UP TO the end.

A woman from Chicago said she wasn't coming because she didn't have a piccolo lyre. Around 11:30 p.m. July 3, a cornet player from Hyde Park who had just heard about the band an hour before asked if he could come.

"You have your own trumpet?" I asked. "I have my own cornet," he said. I knew he was serious. I logged in names and instruments on my computer, trying to keep track of instrumentation and just who was coming. But in the final hours I was too nervous for clerical duties. Instead I drank coffee and worried incessantly about having enough people to field a marching band.

Between phone calls I paced about the house, accomplishing little. "I'll never do this again," I told myself. I was less nervous for the birth of my kids.

Saturday morning was the worst. I was supposed to pick up the key to the Elmhurst College band room the night before. Things got mixed up. I didn't get the key and everybody I called on Saturday was gone. I left desperate messages on their answering machines.

"Couldn't we rehearse outside?" my wife asked. "We could," I said. "But all the drums and Sousaphones are in the band room." I wondered what my blood pressure was at this point.

Then there was the beer. Pavichevich was to deliver it by 7:30 Saturday morning. At 8:00 I was still getting his answering machine.

"None of the clarinet players will have lyres," my wife said. We fumbled with coat hangers and rubber bands, and after a few minutes, came up with something that did a reasonable job of holding clarinet music. I think we made five of them.

Pavichevich showed up at 8:30; so did Doug Beach, who brought the band room key.

A few minutes before nine I went to the college. One drummer and a clarinet player were there already. By 9:10 the cymbal player, bass drummer and another snare drummer showed up and sorted out equipment.

I was so nervous that after opening the band room I stood outside in the parking lot until 9:30, when the rehearsal started.

Just before we went inside, a middle-aged guy with a wife and two kids pulled up in a Taurus station wagon. He grabbed a trombone from the back of the car, and his wife asked where was the best place to see the parade. "After it's over we're leaving for Michigan," she said while turning her head from side to side the way wives of middle-aged guys do, as if to say, "Why is he doing this?"

"Going to Michigan to see your wife's folks?" I asked him as we walked toward the band room.

"How did you know?" he said.

All I can say about the rehearsal is that everybody knew what to do. After hearing the first four bars of "National Emblem," I knew we'd be OK.

We played through the other two marches and walked over to Third and York to wait for the parade to start. Everybody hung out, bought coffee from a nearby gas station and swapped stories about parades and dance jobs they played years before. Or they spoke of their long-dead teachers and high school band directors and what it was like to sit alone with an instrument, struggling with major and minor scales and all the other things musicians have to know.

We were the 25th unit to step off. People yelled and clapped when they saw us. They snapped photos and sometimes leaped out of lawn chairs to follow us for a while. Fathers raised small children to their shoulders so they could wave at us.

Old people cheered the loudest.

The cowboys of Bradley's Drugstore

JIM BRADLEY RAN A DRUGSTORE in Lombard for as long as anybody can remember. He opened it in 1926 and took in $12 the first day. "Maybe I went into the wrong business," he wondered after counting the receipts.

Bradley had five children: four girls, who grew to adulthood, and a son who died at age eight. Some say it was because of his son's death that he always had a soft spot for boys.

The drugstore was a second home for Lombard boys. Bradley saw several generations of them grow to manhood. He referred to his charges as "the cowboys," and throughout World War II, no matter where they were stationed, the cowboys kept in touch.

In 1942 Bradley took out an ad in the Lombard Spectator, which was regularly sent to the troops. About the same length as this column, the ad read like a newsletter:

Dear Fellows:

By this we mean all of you fellows in the Army, Navy, Marines, Air Force, Coast Guard, etc. from this vicinity. We know we owe quite a few of you a letter or card, and we're taking this means of getting even.

We're all feeling fine and keeping pretty busy. We certainly enjoy hearing from you and are sure proud of the collection of snapshots we have of you.

Most of what followed was news about the cowboys. *Lennie, Bob H. and George Spkoizinzkaly (heck! I can't spell) are the latest to sign up. The Army air force welcomed them. Zeke didn't join the Navy because he was afraid they'd clip those gorgeous locks of his...*

Bradley went on for several more paragraphs, then made his offer.

The fellow who is farthest away from Lombard in the armed forces who sends us back this ad cut from the Spectator will receive a $5 bill. We'll give you 60 days to get it back!

Then to make it fair in the states, we'll give another fin to you, but you only got 30 days. Got it straight? That's five bucks for the fellow farthest away from Lombard in the armed forces out of the U.S. and another for the same in the U.S...

Back here we're all eagerly awaiting the day when you'll all come marching home to dear old Lombard. The very best of luck to each and every one of you from each and every one of us at BRADLEY'S DRUG STORE.

Among the many responses, Bradley received the following from Pvt. Robert Kimball, Company A, 8th Battalion, Fort McClellan, Ala.

December 13, 1942

Brad—Or should I say 'Jim and the gals.' I just wanted you to know that I read that ad. ... It was a distinct pleasure to stop in at the old dive every night and get a malted. I think you spoiled me because so far I haven't found one that compares to yours. Of course, the service down here is pretty close to the same that I got at your place...

Tell that sassy, little brown-eyed clerk that I miss her... Can you imagine them trying to make an officer out of me? This school I'm attending now is just a prep school, and if I pass, I'll be sent to Fort Benning, Georgia, for three months. At the end of that time I should be a good case for the booby hatch. Tell her [the clerk] that if she can tear herself away from the horde of men seeking her fair hand that I would like to hear all about the old place...

So long for now—put all that extra money into war bonds because I eat like a horse and don't want to get hungry.
—Bob Kimball

Kimball graduated from officer's candidate school, but his success with the sassy brown-eyed clerk was never documented.

In May 1945, those who didn't come marching home to dear old Lombard were recognized in the Spectator:

"On the following pages of this supplement are reproduced the photographs of 28 Lombard members of the armed forces who up to May 15 had made the supreme sacrifice in this war, according to official reports."

Among the young faces was First Lt. Robert C. Kimball's. He was killed on Luzon on Feb. 20, 1945.

THE OLD NEIGHBORHOOD

Nostalgia for the annoying fifties

THE PLAY "RIVERVIEW: A Melodrama With Music" opened at the Goodman Theatre recently. I haven't seen it, but from what I've read I gather that it is set in the 1940s and 1950s, and that it's a nostalgia-filled piece that brings back memories of the world's greatest amusement park. At least it was the world's greatest to those of us who frequented it.

Having spent a little of my early youth in the forties and the better part of my boyhood in the fifties, I love to reminisce about living in Chicago during those years.

It's easy to forget that we had major social problems then. If I were a 46-year-old black man, I doubt my memories of the 1950s would be filled with warm recollections.

A lot of the big problems we had then are still around, maybe in different forms, but they are still with us. But what about the little things that were as annoying as hell about the fifties that we no longer think about?

• Litter. When was the last time you saw a sign that said "Don't Litter"? People just don't toss garbage wherever they please anymore. In the fifties if you blew your nose, it was OK to drop the used Kleenex on the ground as long as it wasn't in the immediate vicinity of your house. Popsicle sticks and wrappers were routinely pitched from cars, as were beer and pop bottles. Basically, people of the fifties were slobs.

• Smoke. Everybody smoked. In restaurants people not only smoked after dinner, but between courses as well. I had an Irish uncle who routinely fumigated our house with Tip-Top tobacco in his ever-present pipe. After his visits my mother washed the curtains to get rid of the smell of Tip-Top. Our house smelled intermittently of pipe tobacco, but the scent of cigarette smoke was always there. My father knocked off two packs a day of Camel regulars. Living in the fifties was like living in an ashtray.

• Dogs. I rarely see a stray dog now. In the fifties they were plentiful. Seeing a female dog in heat being chased by five or six males was common. Every summer at least one kid in our neighborhood was bitten by a stray. The kid would have to get rabies shots because the dog could never be found. In some neighborhoods dogs roamed in packs and ate garbage from open cans in the alleys.

• Dirt. With a couple of steel mills going full blast, Chicago air was loaded with pollution. Everybody washed walls and ceilings at least once a year. Those on the Southeast Side did it three or four times annually.

Oily soot clung to walls, outlining the strips of lath beneath the plaster, making the room look as if it were decorated with gigantic supermarket pricing codes. To avoid streaking, walls and ceilings had to be wiped down with chemical sponges first, then washed with soap and water.

• Garbage. It's hard to believe that we once lived without plastic garbage bags. In the fifties we emptied garbage into 55-gallon drums that stood in the alley. Of course, the drums rusted and many didn't have covers, attracting millions of huge green garbage flies.

Worse than garbage cans were the small concrete incinerators that sat in back yards. The waist-high cement boxes had a door on top where you dropped in garbage and another at the bottom that opened through a hole in the fence to the alley, where garbagemen shoveled the charred contents into their trucks. People routinely burned newspapers, milk cartons, and anything else that was easily combustible.

Kids sometimes amused themselves by throwing rocks at rusting garbage cans or open concrete incinerators. They liked seeing how many flies they could stir up.

Nintendo wouldn't be invented for another 25 years.

Rapping with jazz was a cool way to grow up

THE ELMHURST COLLEGE JAZZ Festival will celebrate its 25th anniversary at the end of next month. This year's attendance figures will probably top those of all years previous. And we of DuPage can hold our heads high and tell our snooty North Shore friends that we have the tradition of a twenty-five-year-old jazz festival, then ask them how many hip things have happened in Winnetka lately.

But one-upmanship is not the point of America's music. In fact, America's music has no point; that's what makes it so damn appealing.

It's just music. Because my kids own powerful stereo equipment, I listen to rap and heavy metal daily. My house is only 1,800 square feet. How can I escape a couple of Yamaha speakers with 40 watts per channel coursing through them?

I can't, so I listen, hoping that heavy metal and rap, like all other trials, will eventually pass.

Laced into the lyrics of both are social messages. Just what I need when I want to relax—a twenty-two-year-old millionaire with wind-tunnel hair telling me that life can be pretty unfair.

Or a guy with a clock tied around his neck informing me that blacks and whites should get along or that conditions in our inner cities are deplorable.

Unlike my kids and the kids I grew up with, I listened to jazz all through my high school years. I still can't figure out why.

My parents weren't interested in it, and except through recordings, I knew no jazz musicians, and none knew me.

But each night I got into bed with my Heathkit transistor radio, which was about the size of an accordion, and found Sid McCoy, who hosted a late-night jazz radio show.

I listened until I fell asleep. Chicago had some other great jazz radio shows, too. WAAF was a local commercial jazz radio station whose programs were hosted by Dick Buckley, Studs Terkel and Marty Faye.

There was also the unique "Daddy-O's Jazz Patio." Daddy-O spoke in rap verses long before there were rap verses.

Most of the kids my age grew up believing in the standard black stereotypes. My stereotypes were different, though.

I thought every black person was hip. Hipness was something they were born with—they didn't have to acquire it by listening to records and reading Down Beat, like I did.

When I was seventeen, I was stopped for speeding on the Outer Drive by a black cop. "Goin' a little fast there, weren't you?" he said looking at my license.

"Hey man, what do you think about Miles and Coltrane?" I asked, hoping to show him that he wasn't dealing with just any stupid white kid. And also hoping he would forget about the speeding violation.

"Miles who?" he asked, then gave me a ticket. I was crushed. Years later I told that story to a black friend and jazz musician.

"I really like that story," he said. He had me retell it a few times for others. I wondered, but never asked, if he grew up thinking all white people were born accountants.

Those memories of being young and listening to jazz are nice to have now.

If you have any, or have even a passing interest in America's original art form, save a few hours the weekend of February 28 and get over to Hammerschmidt Chapel at Elmhurst College.

To celebrate the festival's 25th anniversary, jazz greats including Terry Gibbs, Bobby Shew and Clark Terry will appear at various sessions.

And if you get stopped for speeding on your way there, don't use that Miles and Coltrane story.

In the days before air conditioning, peace was found in a cool basement

I COULDN'T SLEEP. WHEN I stepped out to get a paper at 5:30, the thermometer at the bank was already at 78. Hot temperatures don't bother me that much these days; my house has central air, and so does the office where I work. It's just a matter of coping with the forty-minute commute in an unair-conditioned car. Things were not always this way, though. When I was a kid, only a few people in our neighborhood had air conditioning. My family could afford a couple of window units, but my father considered them appropriate only for motel rooms.

Within walking distance of our house lived an uncle who rented the second floor of a brick two-flat. My father and I sometimes visited him on summer nights. In fact, those were the only times we visited him; my father never took me there when the temperature was less than 85.

On those visits we sat in my uncle's living room with my aunt, who never drank beer, just highballs—a drink my father thought was consumed only by people who put on airs. He and my uncle drank Atlas-Prager from quart bottles.

My father hated that beer, not because of its taste, but because of a radio commercial that advertised it. A German band played in the background while somebody like Sgt. Schultz from "Hogan's Heroes" sang in his best Katzenjammer German:

"Ja, Ja, oom-pa-pa, Very much good for thirsty, Dat Atlas-Prager Beer!" "Turn the damn thing off," my father said every time it came on the air, unless it was during a Sox game.

During those nights at my uncle's, my father never let his taste in beer be known; he drank Atlas-Prager.

"Be glad you don't have to live there. At least we've got a cool basement," my father always said after we departed my uncle's.

"That heat would kill me. I don't know how they can stand it," my mother said whenever she accompanied us on those visits.

In the view of those in the neighborhood, my father was clearly the superior man. My father owned a bungalow; my uncle rented an apartment. My father had a Chicago Park District administrative job; my uncle was an armed guard for Brinks. Most revealing of all: My father drove Oldsmobiles; my uncle, Pontiacs.

Things change. My uncle was promoted and left behind the Brinks truck to labor daily in an office. He promptly bought a three-quarter-ton window air-conditioner for his apartment and no longer pulled on quarts of Atlas-Prager but instead sipped Miller High Life, "the champagne of bottled beers." His wife graduated to a better grade of whiskey in her highballs.

We visited them less often, and after my uncle bought a Buick, we hardly visited them at all. But when we did, my father always commented on the air conditioner. "Did you hear the racket that thing makes? How the hell can anybody sleep with that going on?"

Eventually, though, my father gave in to progress. During a hot spell he drove to Polk Bros. and bought a window unit. "It takes 220," he whispered out of the side of his mouth to anyone interested or disinterested in volts or amperes.

But my uncle had bought a house in Westchester. "It's got a screened-in porch and central air. The damn thing is hooked to the furnace," my uncle disclosed while showing us the real estate listing with the price cut out.

We visited them even less often after they moved. Despite our window unit that required 220 wiring, my father rarely left the basement during hot spells.

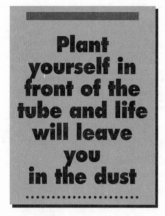

Plant yourself in front of the tube and life will leave you in the dust

MY IRISH GRANDMOTHER lived in the same city neighborhood from the time she came to this country until shortly before her death. In her eighty-four years she never drove a car or ate fast food—two things I still admire her for. Her neighborhood wasn't anything great. Her second-floor flat was on a commercial street; trucks and buses rolled by incessantly.

After my grandfather died, she lived there alone for a long time. As a kid, I sometimes stayed with her during the summer. When she got too old to shop for herself, she called the store at the corner and they sent up a kid with her groceries. Or if I was staying with her, she sent me for her few things. Although she lived alone, she didn't spend her days pining away the hours in front of a television set. She never owned one but did have daily visitors. Late in the morning the mailman came in and gave my grandmother her letters, for which she rewarded him by pouring three fingers of Bushmill's. He then consecrated it, holding it at eye level in the midday light streaming through the lace curtains.

"To you," he said, nodding in my direction as I sat at the dining room table reading the latest installment of Alexander Botts in the Saturday Evening Post. The mailman repeated his nod, this time toward my grandmother, told God to bless her, then finally drank the whiskey and launched into the news of the day.

Even as a kid I was amazed at his ability to tell stories about ordinary people and make their lives seem important. To me his characters were more real and far more entertaining than *The Man in the Iron Mask, The Three Musketeers* or anything else from the young-adult section of the public library.

"That man could charm the birds from the trees," my grandmother said each time after he left.

In the late afternoon Mrs. Mitchell came up for tea. She and my grandmother had known one another in Ireland. Although friends for seventy years, they never referred to each other with first names. They were always Mrs. Mitchell or Mrs. Dunne. My grandmother brewed a pot of Tetley's, measuring the tea in fistfuls as she dropped it into the pot. She then relayed the mailman's story to Mrs. Mitchell, careful to get all the details right. Talking in thick brogues, the ladies gained comfort and strength from each other's company. It didn't matter that their conversations were punctuated with long pauses.

"He's an odd one," Mrs. Mitchell said.

"Indeed he is," Mrs. Dunne replied three minutes later. The two then reflected on his oddness for several more minutes.

Mrs. Murphy, the neighborhood insomniac, came by each night at 10. She wasn't reflective like Mrs. Mitchell or my grandmother. Instead of silence, her conversations were punctuated with unending profanities. She was famous throughout the neighborhood; as a young woman she once booted a local flasher in the sweetbreads. She lovingly referred to FDR as "that crippled bastard," but she always called my grandmother Mrs. Dunne.

As I now look at my grandmother's life, I marvel at its richness. Had she sat in front of a television like so many of us, she would have missed the mailman's eloquent stories or the daily visits from those two old Irish ladies.

This weekend is Elmfest '90 in downtown Elmhurst. We have a chance to break from our suburban dullness and spend some time with one another. Don't turn on the television for a few days. Get down there and visit with your neighbors, tell stories, and, as the posters instruct, "Celebrate your German heritage." My Irish grandmother would be proud.

So would Mrs. Mitchell and Mrs. Murphy.

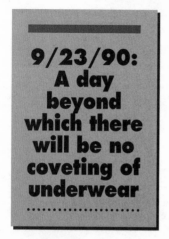

**9/23/90:
A day
beyond
which there
will be no
coveting of
underwear**

I FINALLY BECAME SUCCESSFUL on Sunday afternoon, September 23, 1990. I'm one of those fortunate few who has reached his life's goal. To some this may mean owning a string of Atlantic City gambling casinos or at least a Mercedes-Benz with Vanity plates. Others might consider themselves successful after raising a house full of kids who manage to stay out of the pokey. Still others view success as having enough money to live a major portion of their lives without working.

For me success is owning all new underwear. Forget everything else, this is making it. There are those who need a Honda Acura and a leather bomber jacket or a $500,000 house and a trophy wife to feel successful. Give me a 100 percent combed cotton V-neck undershirt (size 2XL) and shorts that don't bind or experience waistband roll-over and I'm a happy camper.

Odd that so little would make me so happy, but hey, why get goofy over unobtainable goals or wind up in electroshock therapy because you never achieve the one thing in life you really want? Set your goals low enough and you can't fail. But even this low goal has taken me the better part of forty-five years to achieve.

It started when I was a kid. Across the street from us lived an elegant and refined man. Mr. Beauchamp owned a brick two-flat, had a Marion bluegrass lawn and always wore Arrow shirts and dress pants. Even more impressive, he never drank beer but could make any mixed drink in the "Bartender's Guide" from memory. Obviously, a man of the world.

Every few weeks my mother or father glommed on to a new morsel of information about Beauchamp's lifestyle.

"He's French," my mother whispered. "Just like Maurice Chevalier, and I heard he just bought an electric lawn edger."

"He owns stocks," my father once confided. "And if he

stopped working tomorrow, he could go on living in that two-flat forever."

But to us there was nothing as impressive as one of my mother's disclosures. "I was over there while his wife was ironing and I found out that he dates his underwear."

"Whadaya mean, he takes it out to dinner and a show every Saturday night?" my father joked.

"No," my mother informed. "He writes the month and year that he buys all his underwear right on the neck band or waistband with laundry marker, and then after three years he tosses it and starts over with all new stuff."

My father, who was considered quite dapper by neighborhood standards because he regularly bought clothes at Bond's State Street store, was speechless. It was then that I decided that at some point in my life I would emulate Mr. Beauchamp and buy all new underwear at once.

But it wasn't as easy as I thought. Whenever I had the time, I didn't have the money and vice-versa. Finally, I put aside both. While others watched the Bears game Sunday, I pursued 2XL undershirts in the men's department at Sears. Typical of most retail establishments, sizes only run through extra large. But Sears has a little room off to the side with the words "Big and Tall" displayed overhead. Let's face it, though, it's not really for tall men. Two other fat guys and I pawed at the packages of underwear, I got the last 2XLs. It didn't matter if the Bears won or lost.

I spent the rest of the day writing 9/23/90 in laundry marker on my new underwear. Mr. Beauchamp would like that.

No tearing hair out at Uncle Pat's funeral

JUST WHEN I HAD PLANNED TO spend a couple of weeks lolling about Azerbaijan, doing the tourist thing, playing a hand or two of bezique at the local Shiite Moslem Reading Room, I picked up the morning paper and saw these real intense Azerbaijanis generating pungent body odor by blasting one another with automatic weapons and lobbing hand grenades.

A few days later things got worse. In the Azerbaijan capital of Baku, named after a fruit drink, one million people showed up to bury the dead from the street fighting of the past couple of days. I quote from a Tribune news story: "Black-clad women wailed and tore wildly at their hair and clothes; men beat their chests and chanted as the funeral throng marched through the Azerbaijan capital in traditional Shiite Moslem fashion."

And herein lies the difference between us and them. We of the U.S., while criticized by other countries for our loutish, uncouth behavior, mourn with more dignity than people of any other culture. French waiters may look down their sniveling little Gallic noses at us, but when it comes to planting the deceased, at least we get it over with and take a pass on the histrionics.

If you sat in front of the TV set the day of JFK's funeral, you saw thousands of grieving citizens wiping tears from their eyes or just reflecting on the immensity of it all. But I can't recall a single news story of people tearing at their hair and clothes or beating their chests. OK, maybe some Americans got a little carried away when Elvis bought the farm; a housewife or two tried to jump into the crypt with him. But you have to understand that these were not normal housewives, these were women who had spent most of their lives listening to rock music. Those reactions were mild compared to the time the Ayatollah went to that big rug bazaar in the sky. What were all those guys doing slapping themselves on the noggin for several days?

Doesn't Iran have enough problems without three-fourths of its work force phoning in sick with headaches? A really weird funeral was Hirohito's. After he died the Japanese took a couple of months just to make arrangements. It's no big deal, all they had to do is call an undertaker and a florist. And these are the people who accuse Americans of being lazy.

Probably the strangest funeral in this country was that of my Irish uncle. There wasn't any money left for flowers after the family had hired an accordion player for three nights of the wake. The deceased's wife, a woman who had worked for many years as a store detective until she was caught stealing from shoplifters, hit upon a novel plan. A couple of days before the burial she drove out to the cemetery and lifted numerous floral arrangements from fresh graves. She then decorated the funeral parlor with them. At the dinner afterward a couple of the deceased's brothers got into a heated argument over a soured get-rich-quick scheme, a chinchilla ranch that had gone horribly wrong. A fight broke out and police were called.

The fact that my dead uncle's name was Pat and one of the floral pieces said "Farewell Vito" no longer bothered anybody.

Paying one's respects not what it used to be

M Y MOTHER'S IDEA OF AN evening out was to hit two wakes in the same night. She and my father scoured death notices daily to see if there was anyone they knew even vaguely who had passed. They then would drive anywhere in the Chicago area to express their condolences.

But my father never expressed anything. He entered a funeral home and headed straight for the smoking room, where he worked his way through a pack of Camels while my mother and I expressed our condolences.

My father's greatest talent was understanding Chicago's North Side street-numbering system. "Diversey is twenty-eight hundred," he'd say as we left our South Side home heading for yet another wake.

"Your father knows everything," my mother whispered, astonished at his ability to pinpoint east-west streets north of the Loop.

I am reminded of these things because of the passing this week of my wife's mother. My cousin and her husband, who live in Beverly, showed up at the Glen Ellyn wake. "Did you call them?" my wife asked.

"Didn't have to," I said. "They read the death notices."

It's true. My family has always headed for the obit page first. And not only do they look for familiar names, they read every death notice hoping to glom onto a thread of historical lint. "He was second cousin once removed to the onetime Park District comptroller, who was connected with the mayor's nephew," they say, then mentally file the information for retrieval several decades from now.

In recent years, wakes have become sensible affairs, usually a single evening followed by a morning funeral. It wasn't always that way.

In the late 1950s my father was displayed for three nights and had an endless chain of visitors. "He came to all my family's wakes," people at his visitation said, although my father really didn't.

He only drove my mother and me to wakes, while he hid in the smoking room or took a few of the bereaved out for a beer.

Not content with three nights of a wake and a seven-block-long funeral procession, my family fed everyone after my father's departure.

Initially, my mother ordered 150 sandwiches from a local caterer, which were delivered the morning of the funeral.

My family's conception of a sandwich and the caterer's differed.

The caterer's 150 sandwiches were polite little squibs of rolled bread and chicken salad. Though deeply hurt by the loss of her son, my grandmother injected herself into the situation. "There ain't nothin' here," she said. "They'll think we're a bunch of pikers."

My mother only cried.

"Call Mandy," my grandmother finally ordered.

Mandy was a distant German aunt of remarkable girth who thought nothing of preparing food for sixty or seventy. "I'll come on the bus," she said. "In the meantime, pick up some stuff for me."

Mandy dictated a list that began with twenty loaves of unsliced Lithuanian rye bread and ended with five pounds of salted and five pounds of unsalted butter. The middle of the list contained, among other things, liver sausage, veal sausage and pickled tongue.

The miracle of the loaves and fishes was a warm-up lap compared with Mandy working alone that morning. She served at least 120 and nobody thought we were pikers.

"What happened to the 150 sandwiches from the caterer?" my mother asked when the day was finally over.

"I had to eat somethin' while I made all this stuff," Mandy said.

6

JAZZMEN, CHECK-KITERS AND LOVERS

A serenade in passing for a lifetime love

H E CALLED AROUND 10 LAST night. It was the first time we had talked in almost a year. At one time I idolized him. That was when I was young and wanted to be a famous jazz musician. He was that, a famous jazz musician. When I was in high school I owned every recording of his. I didn't want to be like him; I wanted to be him. At one point he gave up all his fame and went to Hollywood to write film music. He was successful at that, too. He stayed there eighteen years, writing music for film and television.

Once in a while I'd see his name roll by on the credits of a TV program. Seeing his name made me remember what it was like to be in high school and dream about playing jazz for a living.

He grew tired of his life in Hollywood and moved back to the Midwest and made a comeback as a performer. For a time he considered writing a book about his life. It would be remarkable. He and a few others defined jazz in the early fifties and sixties.

I edited a magazine interview he did and called him several times to check facts. We felt comfortable with one another and eventually he asked me to look at his book.

The first chapter wasn't about his youth spent learning an instrument. Nor was it about his early years in New York playing with Miles Davis or numerous other professional successes. It was about his wife. The chapter described how she accompanied him on a tour of Japan and how, while he left her at a hotel to perform in another city, she became ill. He canceled the tour and flew her back to the States.

For a while he and I spoke regularly about the book. One afternoon he called me. "I've decided to not go through with the book," he said. He listed a number of reasons: professional commitments, the chance that the book might never sell, the time it would take him away from musical compositions. He concluded his list with the words, "I owe this time to my wife."

We still called one another every couple of months. "She's doing better," he said from time to time. "We're hoping things turn around."

Our conversations grew less frequent, but always concluded with me saying, "If you're ever in Chicago, give me a call so we can meet in person."

We had never met face-to-face but over the years had spent hours on the phone. When he called last night, he told me that his wife had passed on months before. "Some people never have what I had," he said. "We were married for 43 years."

Despite our recent obsession with family values, little is mentioned about men who love the same woman for a lifetime. "I've been feeling sorry for myself," he said. "Instead of being thankful for the time we had together, I've been dwelling on the last three years when she was sick. But I'm through that now. I've recorded an album that I dedicated to her. It's just me and a rhythm section, and it's all ballads. I never did anything like that before. It comes out in September."

I didn't ask if he thought about resuming his autobiography. The album will say more than the book ever could.

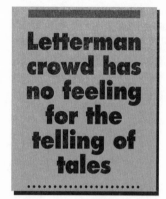

Letterman crowd has no feeling for the telling of tales

M Y IRISH UNCLE CAN REALLY tell stories. If any person on the face of the earth deserves his own television show or at least a guest shot with Johnny Carson, he does. But life deals some strange hands, and my uncle wound up driving a truck for most of his adult years, never even getting his name in a newspaper, much less on a marquee. Nonetheless, to the delight of relatives and friends, he regularly plied his trade at family wakes and weddings. His stories were the best I have ever heard.

The world is full of comedians. There's Richard Pryor and Robin Williams, the self deprecating Rodney Dangerfield and numerous others possessing various degrees of comedic talent. But they don't hold a candle to my Uncle Steve. Comedians tell jokes or use gag lines. They are masters of the quick laugh—low humor and cheap theatrics are their stock in trade. They punch and jab, they shock and ridicule, but my Uncle Steve is a teller of stories with length and breadth, stories of truth. And they aren't the product of Hollywood gag writers. Instead they are real events that occurred in his life or the life of someone he knew. They are so good that you could write them down and sell them.

As a kid when we had family gatherings, my mother always called me inside, "Your uncle is going to tell a story," she said.

"Well you know..." he began in low, dulcet tones as we sat there drinking in each word.

His stories had form. They began with an initial exposition, had a lengthy development section, and were followed by a recapitulation in which he wove together the various elements he had spilled before us. He never went for the cheap laugh. Even if a gag were lying in front of him, he would step over it. His was a higher calling. I memorized those stories: how he paid a black janitor to teach him tap dancing in the basement of Johnny Coulon's gym; his first day on the job with an asphalt patch crew; an X-ray technician telling him that he had long lungs. Each was unique.

Last Sunday when I visited him, there was no storytelling. "Crisis in confidence," his wife said. He had taken a part-time job working in an office with under-thirty upscale types.

"They don't think I'm funny," he confessed. "I've been telling stories for over seventy years and these kids don't think I'm funny."

A few days previous he and his wife had attended a company dinner during which he attempted the telling of a story. "They didn't even pay attention to me," he said. "They just went on talking like I wasn't there."

"These were young kids who were raised with television. They probably never heard anybody tell a story before," his wife comforted. "I think that's what they call cocooning."

"Yeah," I said. "They probably rent videos every weekend and think David Letterman is funny. Maybe if they saw you on television they'd get it."

This brought him little cheer. The thought that there are whole generations of people who have never heard somebody tell a real story weighed heavily on him. I could see that the experience of eating dinner with the yups had forever changed him, and there would be no more stories.

"Where ya been all afternoon," my kid asked as I returned home from my visit.

"Babe Ruth's retirement party," I said.

Soft nights, soft women and old Engine No. 1167

IT WAS OUR WEEKLY RITUAL: One of us would call the other every Sunday morning. He wasn't a blood relative, but we had always been close. I made it a point to see him as often as possible, which wasn't real regular since he had moved to central Florida. Because he was in his eighties and was terrified of flying, it was my job to do the traveling. My wife had relatives in Miami and the kids wanted to see the Epcot mess, so we decided to pile into the car and make one grand swing through the Sunshine State.

After spending a few minutes with him, it was obvious he could no longer live alone. I sent the wife and kids to view the future courtesy of Walt Disney while I stayed with the old man and dealt with the past. The mornings of the next few days were occupied with finding a place for him. He wasn't sick, just too old to make it alone anymore.

In the afternoons we'd sit together in his apartment filled with newspapers. We drank beer with an occasional shooter of his favorite, Old Fitzgerald. He told me his stories. I had heard them all before, but this time it seemed important that I grasp every nuance and detail. For years he had knocked around the country, working at different jobs—tool-and-die maker, linotype operator, gunsmith. But he was most proud of a brief stint as a locomotive fireman on the Sante Fe.

"I worked on a Mallet," he bragged. "Two boilers, 12 drive wheels." He then instructed me in the uniqueness of the Mallet Compound Steam Engine. He spoke of being young and working with men and of the immensity of the engine.

"A she-devil," he called her as he explained how she singed his nostrils and pulled the air from his lungs as she sucked up the steel ribbon on steep grades and how coal exploded on the end of his shovel as he fed her belly. He also spoke of soft nights spent with soft women in open fields. We'd stop drinking and talking around 5 o'clock and eat a couple of TV dinners. At 9 he put on pajamas, removed his dentures and slowly slipped under the sheets, placing a sponge between his knees because he was old and worn and if he didn't, his knees rubbed on one another and would ache.

On the fifth day we found him a place. He gave me his Ford and I headed north preoccupied with the thought of a man who plied prairie and mountain in the Mallet she-devil, now living under a suspended ceiling in a Florida rest home.

Three days after I got back they called. Just before the funeral the preacher asked if there were any facts about the deceased's life that should be incorporated into the eulogy. I told him of the Atchison Topeka and Santa Fe Railway and Engine No. 1167.

When the time came, the preacher explored the 23rd Psalm and spoke of the importance of sincerity. No mention was made of the creations of Anatole Mallet or the men who gave them life.

I never visited his grave again, but every now and then I drive out to the railway museum in Union, Illinois. I look at the Mallet Compound now still and think of the old man who slept with a sponge between his knees, once young and making love to women in open fields. He would like that.

My mother knew you can't fly on one wing

"I WANT TO BE PIPED OUT OF church," my mother told me countless times when speaking of her funeral. She was never morose in discussing her final arrangements. After all, she was Irish, a race that cries at life and laughs at death. A bagpiper to conclude her funeral mass seemed reasonable.

Three years ago she handed me an envelope with the words "To be opened in the event of my death" typed on it. I took it home and immediately disobeyed her wishes, opening it while hoping it would say something like, "My Dear Son, all these years I've concealed my wealth from you. I'm worth several mil. Order yourself a Jag."

It said no such thing. Enclosed in the envelope was a $100 bill. The accompanying note spelled our her wishes. "Dear Jack, Buy a drink for everyone who comes to my funeral. Love, Mom."

That was my mother, a woman of funny stories and good times. When she passed on last week, several people asked if they could make a donation to her favorite charity.

"Spend your money on having a good time," I told them. "My mother was not a woman of causes, charitable or otherwise."

My cousin and her husband sat up with my wife and I the night my mother passed on.

"Is there anything we can do?" my cousin asked.

"The undertaker should take care of everything," I told her. "But where the hell are we going to get a bagpiper?"

"Don't worry," my cousin said. "We'll take care of that."

My cousin, who is third-generation Irish, married a man who is second-generation Irish. They regularly employ a piper for first communions, confirmations and all other social events. I cannot remember attending one of their gatherings when a bagpiper didn't make a pass or two through the house.

"You had better clear it with the church first," my cousin's husband cautioned. "Sometimes pastors don't allow pipes in church." My cousin's husband was experienced in such matters. He briefly studied to be an Irish Christian Brother but gave up religious life to pursue Democratic politics.

"What's the pastor's name?" he asked.

"Can't remember," I said. "But I think he's Italian."

"Might be trouble," he said.

Late the following morning my cousin called. "We've got the piper," she said and then informed me that this was indeed the family's regular piper and not a mere apprentice. She listed his credentials and named a few of the Irish Democratic notables he had piped to the Elysian fields.

"I talked to your priest," my cousin's husband whispered before the funeral mass.

"He's not my priest," I told him. "I'm Protestant."

"Doesn't matter," my cousin's husband instructed. "The priest said that he's uncomfortable with bagpipes in church. So I reminded him that this day is neither about his comfort nor mine, but it did little good. He doesn't want the piper in church. We'll have him play when we come out with the casket."

And so it was. We finished the funeral mass and walked behind the pallbearers and casket into the brightness of the day as the piper played "The Wearing of the Green."

After the burial we honored the deceased's other wish and drank together in a South Side bar.

Two days before as I searched my mother's apartment for her favorite rosary I found another envelope. This one tucked in her bedside copy of Brendan Behan's *Confessions of an Irish Rebel*. "To be opened in the event..." was typed on it, and inside was another $100 bill but without the first post-funeral instructions: "Buy everybody a second drink," it said.. "They can't fly on one wing."

An unexpected tradition passes to a new keeper

MOTHER WAS A WRITER. I knew nothing of this. She passed on a month ago and left behind several spiral-bound notebooks of her work. Her writings fit no accepted form. None of them are the length of the shortest newspaper column, and they follow no literary format. They are nothing more than written snapshots of her life and the life of her family.

"She should have kept a diary," my wife said after looking at some of the notebooks. My mother should have, but she couldn't; she was not a woman of schedules and organization. Her notebooks bear this out. None of them contain a complete date. A writing might begin with the day and month but will not include the year. Or it may begin with simply "Monday" with no month or year following.

The pages of the notebooks don't proceed in any order. My mother was not the kind of person who finished one thing before starting on the next. She had her spiral-bound notebooks distributed throughout her apartment and when moved to write, grabbed the closest one. And she didn't fill every consecutive page. Sometimes she wrote things in the middle or back of an otherwise unused book.

This was a woman who never packed before leaving on vacations. "I'll buy clothes when I get there," I heard her say more than once as I drove to O'Hare to watch her board a departing flight with only the clothes on her back and a small purse. That is how she traveled through all of life.

Her writings were no different. A notebook might contain a draft of a letter to her grandson: "...hope all your teen years will be as happy and as much fun as you can possibly enjoy. Birthday cards seemed so yucky and too much money ($1.00 for a card— no, no, no), so I just included the price of the card in your check. I'd rather you would have the money than Hallmark."

Or a report of a medical test: "I was put on a table and my head was covered by the upper part of the machine. The instructions were to lay perfectly still, absolutely no movement in any part of the body. I dozed off for a few minutes despite the sounds the machine made. I've been feeling fine, and I look normal (or so I think) but I'm tired of medicines. I wish I had the guts to stop taking them. Oh, well, lots of people are worse off."

More important than the notebooks, though, are the hundreds of vignettes of family history, which my mother collected and retold without ever writing down. In her last months she made sure I heard every sliver of family goings and comings she could come up with.

"Your great-grandfather on your father's side made a ton of money in the saloon business during Prohibition. His daughter's husband was a carpenter at a government warehouse where they stored confiscated booze. He went to work every day with an empty toolbox, filled it with Canadian whiskey and dropped it off at the saloon each night. The old man sold it for 50 cents a shot and people stood four-deep at the bar to buy it. He put all his money in Bain banks and was playing cards with old man Bain the night before his banks failed. Your great-grandfather lost everything in the crash."

Some families pass wealth from one generation to the next. Mine has passed stories, photographs and four shopping bags full of spiral-bound notebooks. All this has come to me, and now, I'm the keeper of the family's history. Guess I should fill a few notebooks of my own.

**Alone
and
broke
in
Gotham**

I'VE TOLD THE STORY A THOU-
sand times. In 1970, when I was in
the Navy, my ship docked in New
York City. We had finished a long
exercise at sea, and higher-ups
thought it would be a good idea to let
1,400 sailors have a go at the Big
Apple. I had about forty bucks to my
name and three days to spend it.
Even then that was pin money in
Manhattan.

Besides my financial problems, I had no civilian clothes along.
The Vietnam era wasn't the best of times to walk around Fun City
or anywhere else dressed like Gene Kelly in a dopey 1940s musical. I didn't have cab fare, so each day I hiked it from the ship
into deepest Manhattan.

By my third day of liberty I had sore feet and was down to
my last five bucks. While standing on the corner of Third Avenue
and 42nd waiting to cross with the light, a guy looked at the lyre
insignia on my sleeve and said, "I used to be a Navy musician."
We talked. He was 20 years my senior, but we knew a lot of the
same people. He bought me lunch at Schrafft's and then got me a
house seat at Radio City Music Hall while he played the show
there. Afterward we went to supper, and he picked up the tab
again. The guy had a million stories, and I felt that even after six
hours with him I was only scratching the surface.

Obviously, for a sailor alone with no money in New York City,
this was a lucky break—probably the highlight of my Naval
career. I had intended to drop him a line and thank him, I could
have called the New York Musicians Local for his address, but I
always put it off and never did. A few years later I was back in
New York and asked for him at Radio City. The security guard told
me that they no longer did daily shows and that if I wanted to see
the musicians I should return in a few months for a special Easter
performance. I didn't try to get in touch with him after that.

Months grew into years; I had left the Navy, married, had children and tried a couple of different careers, but a day didn't go by that I didn't think of that guy, a complete stranger who had spent the better part of a day entertaining a sailor who was broke and lonely. I often told people about that day in New York and the irony of finding someone like him in what everybody perceives as the capital city of jerkdom.

Last Friday morning I was on the phone with a man in California. Somehow we began talking about New York. I told him my story of being in service and down to my last five bucks when out of nowhere this trombone player from Radio City Music Hall pops for a couple of meals and gets me into a stage show.

"I knew him," the voice said on the other end of the phone. "He was always doing stuff like that, a real prince."

"I'm going to drop him a line," I said. "I'll call Local 802 and get his address. I've put it off for too long now."

"You're a little late," he said. "He died two weeks ago." This is a tough one. I write for a living, and I've had twenty years to compose a short note. But because I'm such an important person with so many important things to do, I never took pen in hand and wrote the words, "Thank you."

After I got off the phone with California I went into the bathroom and took a long look at the guy in the mirror. He didn't deserve that day in Manhattan.

If the check floats, it's probably Eddie's

EDDIE KITED CHECKS. EVERYbody does it once in a while. You need a load of groceries just before payday, so you write a bad check to the supermarket and hope your paycheck hits the bank before the floater.

Eddie's problems were different, though. I first met him in 1970, when he had two jobs. Eddie was pulling down fifty big ones, which isn't bad today, but in '72 it was a small fortune. Despite his wealth, he drove an eight-year-old car, bought his clothes at Sears and didn't run around with women, at least that I knew of. He lived with his folks so he wasn't dumping big bucks into rent or hefty mortgage payments. None of us who hung around with him could figure out what he did with his money.

"Maybe he plays the ponies," I once mused. But his other friends thought little of the idea. Something didn't ring true about Eddie, racetracks and bookies. But Eddie went through far more that $50,000 a year. He had four checking accounts, which he used to cover his bad checks.

Say he wrote a $500 floater on Monday with a check from bank A. On Tuesday he'd deposit a $500 check from bank B in Bank A. The following day he would cover the check from bank B by depositing a check from bank C. Of course, the $500 never really existed. The whole thing was done on paper. After a few weeks, Eddie deposited real money, so he could get on with other schemes.

His kiting had several variations. He didn't necessarily press all four checking accounts into service. Often he traded checks with friends, especially out-of-town friends.

"Don't deposit my check for a couple of days," Eddie told them. "I need the float time." And so it went.

At times Eddie used cash advances on his credit cards. When things got really desperate, he charged expensive items from Marshall Field's and sold them to people in the neighborhood.

"I need cash to keep floating," he once told me.

"But what are you floating?" I asked, never understanding how a single guy living on $50,000 could get into such dire straights. He never answered my question.

"I guess I'm just addicted to kiting," he confessed.

It certainly occupied his time. He spent every spare minute chasing down checks or cooking up schemes to give him yet another day of float time. He once showed me how he used a cigarette to burn off part of the computer code on a check.

"They can't use the computer to cancel it," he said. "Somebody has to walk it through, so it gives me an extra day or two before it hits my bank." The man was a virtuoso. But in 1980 it caught up with him. It wasn't through carelessness or inattention on Eddie's part that caused everything to unravel. His mother called the presidents of banks A,B,C and D and turned her son in.

Eddie was in deep by then. He had to borrow $30,000 from relatives to stop the float, turn all his checks and credit cards in and go cold turkey. The alternative was to spend time in the Big House.

I haven't seen him in years, but I heard that now he's finally married. Yesterday I sat down to lunch with a friend of his. "How's Eddie," I asked.

"Deep trouble," he said. "His wife is a shopper and likes her plastic way too much." I knew what was coming next. "Eddie's kiting again," he said.

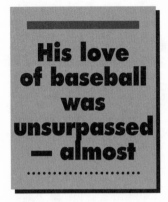

His love of baseball was unsurpassed — almost

I'VE NEVER KNOWN ANYONE who loved baseball more than he did. For more years than I can remember, his grandson and my son played ball together.

The grandson was a gifted player; that was apparent from the start. The kid was a batting technician.

"He's got quick wrists and can really get around on the ball," I heard others say more than once.

It was true. In all the years I watched the kid play, I can't remember him striking out more than a few times. And in those same years, I can't recall the kid's grandfather ever missing a baseball game. His grandmother didn't miss any either. They were always early. She'd push her husband's wheelchair to where he could see from just the right angle. And then they'd stay until the last out, no matter how long the game went.

There were April games that were so cold that I'd spend half the innings in my car. Yet the old man and his wife never left the field. He wore parkas and scarves and his wife bundled him in blankets in the wheelchair. They always carried a Thermos of coffee and offered me a cup in my retreat. "Can't you take it?" or "What kind of a baseball fan are you?" the old man yelled to me as I headed for the parking lot.

In July and August the team would play on ball diamonds in distant suburbs where fields had no trees or shade of any kind. The air was still and temperatures brutal. Even so, the old man never missed a single inning of his grandson's games.

There were years of traveling teams, tournament teams, post-season teams, trips to Wisconsin. Some months I saw the old man daily. Whenever I pulled up to a strange field, I looked for him to confirm I was at the right place at the right time. He was as much a part of Elmhurst baseball as the coaches and players. It was obvious that he loved baseball, and just as obvious was his love for his grandson.

I often thought of the old man, what he was like when he was young, before the wheelchair. I was always curious about his life but could never bring myself to talk with him about these things. Instead I joked with him about my ignorance of the game, or I accepted his wife's coffee from the Thermos.

My son and his grandson grew toward manhood. Each season their ball-playing moved to higher levels of sophistication. My understanding of the game was always sketchy. But the old man's wasn't. He knew every bizarre rule and its application. When his grandson was younger they traveled to Florida to follow the White Sox spring training games.

My son graduated from high school a year ago and went off to college. His grandson, a year younger, remained at York. I no longer went to high school games and no longer saw the old man in the wheelchair every day. But I did think of him often and of how lucky his grandson was to have a grandfather like him.

There was a time when kids shared their childhoods with their grandparents. Generations of one family lived under the same roof or close enough to one another that grandparents could touch the lives of succeeding generations. Now kids are lucky if they know their own fathers and mothers.

The grandfather passed away in January. If life were fair, he would have lived through one more baseball season to see York win the state Class AA title Saturday. And he would have seen his grandson drive in the winning run.

Maybe he did.

AT THE MOVIES

Movie titles reveal a lot about plot

CAUGHT UP IN THE HYSTERIA of the moment, I had this great idea for an Oscar Column. But then I remembered that I never go to the movies. After all, why should I spend six or seven bucks to sit in a dark room with a bunch of teen-age mouth breathers who snort when they laugh? I can do the same thing at home.

Anyway, the real reason I don't bother going to movies is that a smart guy like me can figure out movie plots from the titles without ever entering a movie theater. It's a rare talent that has something to do with ESP or the fact that I inhaled a lot of oven cleaner as a child.

Of course, most people doubt I can do this until they hear a couple of my plot summaries: *Driving Miss Daisy*—Obviously the story about a black chauffeur in a southern town who packs a high-powered air rifle that he uses to shoot rednecks who mouth off to him at stoplights. He works for an elderly Jewish lady whose daughter tries to seduce him by leaving a trail of saltwater taffy from the kitchen into her bedroom. It doesn't work. Our hero hates saltwater taffy and instead falls for the daughter of the Grand Dragon of the KKK who lives next door and who has been feeding him a steady supply of hush puppies and Moon Pies over the back fence. Things come to a head when our chauffeur wins a 500-mile stock car race and kicks the spleen out of a couple of

New York reporters who have been dogging his future father-in-law over his involvement in a charm school for poor white folks. "I'm just glad he's not Catholic," the Grand Dragon says to his daughter as she and the chauffeur drive off into the sunset with a couple of Moon Pies on the dashboard.

Born on the 4th of July—At long last we have overcome our national guilt and produced our first Vietnam-era musical. The movie begins with our hero getting his draft notice. He becomes depressed and sullen, but his girlfriend cheers him up with a snappy rendition of "You Can't Fake Your Physical." She then tells him to hold a bar of soap under each armpit for several days to elevate his blood pressure to the top floor. Unfortunately, his examining doctor, a product of Montessori medical training, believes that blood pressure can be anything it wants to be. Our hero is welcomed into the Armed Forces with a huge chorus number à la Busby Berkeley. Other songs include "The Westmoreland Blues," "If Only I had Gone to Graduate School," and "Next Time, I'll Be a Girl."

Dead Poets Society—Good horror movies have always been rare. *Out of Africa* being the last one. *Dead Poets Society* is more than just a literary remake of *Friday the 13th*. Here we have the classic plot of a young poet (played by Robin Williams) wanting to write like Walt Whitman. Through a mix-up in time travel, Williams is dropped off at Walden Pond alongside Henry David Thoreau. All is not tranquil as one would expect, though. Ralph Waldo Emerson repeatedly tries to murder Thoreau and submit *Walden* to a publisher as his own work. But wait, things really heat up when Edgar Allan Poe, wearing a hockey mask, drops in with an assortment of rusty surgical instruments. Our young poet's life is saved when Herman Melville, who just happened to be fishing nearby, impales both Emerson and Poe on the same harpoon. Robin Williams returns to the present, swears off ever writing poetry and starts life anew as a technical writer for a software company.

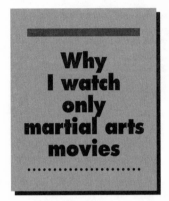

**Why
I watch
only
martial arts
movies**

WHEN I WAS JUST OUT OF high school, movies were important to me. Every time another depressing, Swedish, subtitled flick opened at the local art cinema, I was there. At that time art movies were always European, which meant they had no plots. The actors stared at one another for two or three hours while pondering the meaning of life and all that other stuff Europeans are always pondering. I took dates to these movies, hoping to impress them with my keen intellect and artistic sensitivity. "Fellini's view of life is just like mine," I'd say to an attractive young thing whose father was a sheet-metal fabricator.

Naturally, I never got very far. Women, especially the daughters of sheet-metal workers, aren't enthusiastic about spending their evenings with a guy too stupid to have a good time. Worse still, I drove a Rambler.

Anyway, I eventually grew out of the art-film phase. In fact, for the past several months I have restricted my viewing solely to martial-arts movies. Women can't stand these either. Whenever I return home from Blockbuster Video with another Steven Seagal or Jean-Claude Van Damme movie tucked under my arm, my wife gives me her best "You're Pathetic" look and goes to bed.

Women only like movies in which the main character: a) is a woman who conquers a terminal illness and reunites with her estranged daughter;. b) is a woman who dies of a terminal illness; c) is a man whose girlfriend dies of a terminal illness; d) is an old lady who goes on a long bus ride. Basically, we watch movies that give us something that's missing from our lives. Most women do not have a terminal illness, nor do they take long bus rides. Hence, they watch movies that contain these key elements.

The only reason I watch martial-arts movies is that—and this is hard to admit—I have never been in a fight, not even in high school. But once a drunken Marine took a swing at me when I was defending this country against music both foreign and domestic as a U.S. Navy trombone player. It isn't that I have lacked opportunities to fight. The truth is, I'm a coward. The thought of enduring physical pain sends me into a panic.

But just once I'd like to be Jean-Claude Van Damme and stroll into a fast-food restaurant. The first teenager to chew with his mouth open would get a slap across the face with my instep. Or maybe I would stop by a convenience food store that was being held up. Like Steven Seagal in *Hard to Kill,* I'd disarm two or three robbers with a couple of drop kicks and a mop handle to the groin. That would be living. Forget owning a Mercedes or making a couple hundred big ones a year, I just want to be a tough guy and get even with all the mopes who have made my life miserable.

The next time I'm paying for gas and the guy in front of me wants Lotto tickets, I'll say, "Hey pal, if you want to gamble, go to the track. I'm in a hurry to get to work." Then if he says anything other than "Gee, mister, I'm sorry," I would break his arm in a couple of places and tell him to get professional help with his gambling problem.

Of course, if I were really a tough guy, I'd want to hang out where there are a lot of other tough guys, so I could kick butt on a regular basis. How many fights can I get into at Rotary Club luncheons? Maybe I should try long bus rides.

Move over, Siskel and Ebert

SUMMER'S LAST THREE-DAY weekend is upon us. If you're smart you'll want a few hours off from the traditional Labor Day picnic activities like playing lawn darts or dumping guilt on close family members. Instead, think about retreating to a local movie house, where you can stave off depression or at least escape from loony in-laws and the Jerry Lewis Telethon.

Like most people, while you're there, you'll probably want to see a movie. And because first-run movies cost six bucks a whack, you'll need the advice of a competent movie critic. This is where it gets tough. Movie critics are not like the rest of us. They have studied film, which means they like anything that examines the meaning of life, is depressing and has subtitles. Worse still, they don't pay six bucks to see a movie. In fact, they not only get in free, they are paid thousands of dollars for bashing Charles Bronson and acting as if Jack Nicholson has developed a cure for cancer every time he delivers a line.

Unfortunately, critics often see films before writing about them. This is an unnecessary step that slows down spontaneity and creativity. If they really knew a lot about films, they could write reviews just from the ads.

Take the movie *Lethal Weapon 2*. We know that it stars Mel Gibson and Danny Glover—neither of whom looks like a high ACT score. If you saw *Lethal Weapon 1,* you'd remember that the movie consisted of people blasting one another with automatic weapons, Mel Gibson getting depressed and thinking about suicide and numerous karate kicks tossed in for good measure. Why would *Lethal Weapon 2* be any different? Thus, a movie review without the unnecessary bother of viewing the movie: Hold on to your hats, action fans! Mel Gibson and Danny Glover play two L.A. cops who live on the edge and give us the most gripping police action movie of the summer. A top-notch thriller from beginning to end, this is Glover's best effort yet. His character is developed beyond the shallow one-dimensional type portrayed in *Lethal Weapon 1*. And Gibson shows us that he's more than just another good-looking Chuck Norris. The movie kept me on the edge of my seat a full ninety minutes. Not bad, huh? Let's try *Batman*. I haven't seen that one yet either. I expected something like *Superman,* but boy, was I surprised! *Batman* has all the makings of the movie of the decade. Not just a dumb action film for kids, these characters have scope and breadth and within just a few minutes the viewer is drawn in. The thing I liked best was the look of the movie. Unlike *Superman,* which was comic-book in its approach, *Batman* is deep and cerebral with murky scenes, almost existential in outlook. And then there's the acting. Michael Keaton gives the performance of the decade. Kim Basinger proves that good looks are not detrimental to an actress—those lips of hers look better than ever. And what can be said about Jack Nicholson except that he is the greatest human being in the history of the world. This is an important movie that should be seen by everyone. There you have it, a person who never took a single course in cinema and who never bothered to see the movies he reviewed, writing movie reviews with the best of them. Move over Roger Ebert, Gene Siskel and Nick Pullia. There's a new kid in town.

Great moviegoing gone with the wind

THE WOODS THEATER, LAST OF the Loop's great movie houses, closed Sunday. Not that it really matters much anymore, since most of us now see flicks in suburban shopping malls or on video cassette. But I remember as a teenager in the late fifties taking dates downtown and finding free parking spaces on lower Wacker, or if that didn't pan out, we'd leave my family's Rambler on Columbus and hoof it several blocks over to State and Randolph.

A stone's throw from that corner there were numerous movie theaters to choose from: the State and Lake, the Chicago, the Roosevelt, the Oriental, and of course, the Woods. For these outings, I always wore a blue serge suit from Robert Hall. It cost my folks 40 bucks and came with two pairs of pants. The hardest part of teenage dating was getting out of my own home. Minnie, my German grandmother, managed the household with the thoroughness and efficiency of a Prussian field marshal. Before leaving on a date, I had to undergo her routine interrogation:

"You got money? Keys? Your wallet? An ironed handkerchief? When's the last time you got a haircut? And remember to be a gentleman and treat all girls like they was your mother."

"Jeez, Minnie," I'd say. "This is a lot of trouble to go through to take my mother to the show."

"Accchhh, what do you know?" she'd moan. "Be a gentleman. You'll never regret it."

With the girls I dated, I really didn't need that caution.

The Loop movie houses of those years were genuine palaces. On Friday and Saturday nights they'd be filled with the sons and daughters of working-class parents who had given their kids ironed handkerchiefs and stern warnings to behave like ladies and gentlemen. Despite the fact that they still entertain us, the movies made prior to the sixties were pretty tame by today's standards. The "f" word or even the "s" word never appeared in the scripts—

no nudity, and sex was something only hinted at. When someone was shot, his body parts didn't explode all over the screen.

Art imitates life, and life imitates art. Movies changed. "More like reality" is what they told us—but that was the whole purpose of taking a date downtown, to escape reality. Unfortunately, the audience changed, too. Going to the movies isn't that much fun anymore, especially if you sit near mouth-breathers whose parents never told them to behave like ladies and gentlemen. Most of these kids think they're at home watching a rock video instead of sitting among people who shelled out five or six bucks of their hard-earned money and who would like the simple pleasure of hearing the dialogue.

But that's life in these sophisticated times. Of course, things are tough for today's teen-agers. If your role model during adolescence was Rambo, your social skills would be radically different from someone who idolized Rhett Butler. Oddly enough, the Woods, the movie house that showed *Gone With The Wind* for a solid year in the early forties, closed forever Sunday with a double feature, *Hellbound* and *I'm Gonna Git You Sucka*.

Days and nights on the Schwarzenegger hotline

SCHWARZENEGGER HOTLINE! "Hey, when does Arnold's new movie 'Total Recall' come out?"

If you live in the greater Chicago metropolitan area, it's today, but our advice is to wait a couple of weeks before seeing it. That way the theaters won't be jammed with adolescent iron-pumping geeks.

Schwarzenegger hotline, can I help you?

"Yeah, what was the name of the character that Arnold played in *Running Man?*"

No problem for the Loose Change Schwarzenegger hotline. It was the immortal Ben Richards.

Schwarzenegger hotline!

"Umm, me and my wife are having an argument over the name of the girl that Arnold tries to kill in *The Terminator.*"

Sarah Connor. And don't forget that he starts by trying to eliminate every Sarah Connor in the L.A. phone book.

Schwarzenegger hotline!

"I'll bet you'll never get this one. In what movie does Arnold co-star with Loni Anderson?"

That's a tough one that only real Arnophiles would know. He and Loni Anderson starred in the made-for-TV movie, "The Jane Mansfield Story." Together they had muscles in places where the rest of us don't even have places.

Schwarzenegger hotline!

"What kind of robot is he in *The Terminator?*"

A cyborg. They're robots with steel skeletons covered with human tissue.

I've been manning these phones all night. In case you haven't noticed, Arnold Schwarzenegger, a large Caucasian male who lifts heavy weights, is about to burst into movie theaters everywhere with his latest opus, *Total Recall.* His picture dominates several magazine covers this month, not to mention last Sunday's Tribune Arts section. I guess he is an arteest of sorts. Legions of adolescent boys French curl barbells nightly hoping to achieve some of his total pumposity...

Schwarzenegger hotline!

"I got a bet with one of my friends. In *Raw Deal* what musical masterwork is playing on the stereo when Arnold comes home to his wife who is half-loaded?" That's some bet. The piece on the stereo was Tchaikovsky's "Romeo and Juliet Overture." Later, after she throws a cake at him and passes out in a drunken stupor, Arnold carries her into the bedroom à la Rhett Butler to the strains of the Mozart 21st piano concerto, which was also used in the soundtrack of *Elvira Madigan,* the tragic story of two lovers who kill themselves. Pretty subtle symbolism, huh?

Schwarzenegger hotline!

"In what movie does Arnold utter those immortal words, 'I'll ram my fist into your stomach and break your [expletive deleted] spine?'"

Running Man.

Schwarzenegger hotline!

"Quick! In what movie is Arnold crucified?"

It's in *Conan the Barbarian.* He manages to get off the cross but later critics crucified him for making such a dumb movie.

Schwarzenegger hotline!

"In what movie does Arnold appear with Grace Jones?"

It was none other than *Conan The Destroyer,* the sequel to *Conan the Barbarian.*

Schwarzenegger hotline!

"In what movie does Arnold star in which he doesn't kill any-one?"

Wow! this is a tough one. How about *Twins?*

Schwarzenegger hotline!

"What HBO series has Arnold directed?"

Tales from the Crypt..

Schwarzenegger hotline!

"Hey, which of his movies take place in Chicago?"

The Loose Change Schwarzenegger hotline can only come up with two, *Raw Deal* and *Red Heat.*

Schwarzenegger hotline!

"Isn't there a Schwarzenegger movie where he karate kicks the windshield of a speeding car?"

Whoa, that's Chuck Norris Territory. Arnold can't do karate kicks because his thighs rub together.

MUSIC, MUSIC, MUSIC

Teacher lifts talented musician to greatness

THREE OR FOUR PEOPLE called on Saturday to tell me jazz trumpet great Miles Davis had died. Even though he was a hero of mine since I was a junior in high school, I wasn't saddened by his passing. Miles lived sixty-five years and the way he went at it, it was amazing he got past thirty.

The other kids I hung out with in high school were Dixieland freaks. They listened to a lot of Louis Armstrong and The Dukes of Dixieland, who were very hot in the fifties and sixties. My friends weren't impressed with Miles. "Al Hirt is the best trumpet player in the world," they often said, which was pretty stupid when you think about it.

On one of Hirt's recordings the words, "The Greatest Trumpet Player in the World," were printed across the album cover. "Don't believe everything you read," I told my friends. Even though I was young and stupid and didn't understand much about music, I knew that Miles was into things other than playing louder, higher and faster.

I bought my first Miles album around 1960 or '61. It was "Walkin'," which he made in 1954. I owned several records by Dizzy Gillespie and Charlie Parker prior to my introduction to Miles, and when I first heard *Walkin'*, I was surprised how much space there was in Miles' music, especially after listening to all that be-bop of Parker and Gillespie, where they stuck two chord changes on every beat and played frenetic melodies that jerked around.

It wasn't until a year later, when I bought his "Someday My Prince Will Come" album, which featured tenor saxophonist John Coltrane, that I understood just how hip Miles was and how unhip my friends were. "That tenor sax player sounds like a Mixmaster," they said after I played a few choruses of Coltrane for them. "And anybody could play like that trumpet player." It didn't bother me, though; Miles and Coltrane were my buddies — at least I thought so.

Anyway, Miles has withstood the test of time. When's the last time anybody bought an Al Hirt album? Since the announcement of Miles' death, a string of eulogies has poured forth, and I'm sure they will continue. Even the rap group Public Enemy asked for three seconds of silence in his honor on last week's "Saturday Night Live."

The one thing people forget about musicians is that they are products of their teachers. Jazz musicians have many influences, but somebody gave Miles Davis weekly lessons and taught him how to blow and play scales.

Miles first studied under Elwood Buchanan, his junior high school band director. At that time every jazz trumpeter played like Louis Armstrong or Roy Eldridge, with a fast, wide vibrato that today sounds corny.

Buchanan told Miles to skip the vibrato and play straight, something that distinguished him from the rest of his peers.

In high school, Miles studied with Joe Gustat, a German-American who played first trumpet in the Saint Louis Symphony. I can't imagine what those lessons were like. In his autobiography Miles rendered Gustat his ultimate compliment: "He was a bad [expletive deleted]."

Gustat taught him for $2.50 a lesson, which was a lot of money during the depression. But Miles came from aristocratic stock: his father was a dentist who graduated from Northwestern, and his grandfather owned a farm in Arkansas.

Besides teaching and playing, Gustat also made trumpet mouthpieces. Miles played on nothing else his entire career.

He didn't play a second too long

YOUNG PLAYERS STILL TALK about him and are still influenced by the recordings he made. Philip Farkas, French horn legend, passed away last week in Bloomington, Ind., where he had taught and lived since his retirement from the Chicago Symphony in 1960.

I had interviewed him by phone for a magazine article a few days before his death. He had no intentions of dying—at least that is the image he projected.

But the end comes regardless of intentions or images. I never met Farkas in person but felt we were close. For several months I worked at writing part of a book of his, but that was some time ago. Originally the book was to be a collection of letters written about Farkas by friends and professional associates. The letters were effusive in their praise of him. Several gushed for six or eight pages. Most were heavily edited and drastically shortened. Even so, the he-was-the-most-wonderful-teacher-I-ever-had theme dominated each entry.

But along with the stacks of letters I was supposed to organize and edit were four hour-long cassette tapes. The compiler of all these writings got together with Farkas, a couple of pizzas and several six-packs of beer and recorded the evening.

The tapes were hysterical. Along with playing the French horn better than his contemporaries, Farkas was a master teller of stories. I transcribed each tape word-for-word, arranged them into sections, eventually filling the first 32 pages of his book.

It took a long time to do this and whenever something wasn't clear or needed more details, I called the compiler, who then taped another interview.

The trouble was, I became hooked on Phil Farkas. I never wanted the book to be published because for me, it would be over. There would be no more installments of stories and recollec-

tions of a man born in Elmhurst in 1914, who played his first season as principal horn in the Chicago Symphony in 1936 and who
retired from orchestral playing in his mid-forties for a life of college teaching.

I stalled on the book. I searched the tapes over and over,
looking for some detail that had not been explored. Eventually I'd
find something, call the compiler and start the process anew.

But even so, it came to an end; the book was finally published, and I didn't hear any more stories from Farkas for several
years.

A few weeks ago I was asked to interview anyone who
played in the Chicago Symphony in the 1930s. "Do you have anyone in mind?" my boss asked.

"Yeah," I said. "Phil Farkas."

"You retired at the age I got my first real job," I told Farkas in
our phone conversation. He laughed and said I was still young
and had a lot of life left.

"Players are only remembered for their last performance.
Better to quit five years too soon than to play five minutes too
long," Farkas said, recalling how some of the heroes of his youth
were no longer regarded as great players in their old age.

"You're the Garbo of the French horn," I told him. He liked
that image.

The interview was easy, a forty-five-minute recorded phone
conversation. Farkas sounded fresh and relaxed. He loved to talk
and told me stories I had not heard on the tapes of years before.
He did not sound like a man nearing eighty.

"I still practice the horn every day," he said. He's being buried
as I write this. I was offered a ride to Bloomington to attend the
services but declined. Instead I'll play the tape of that last phone
conversation tonight and maybe drink a few beers in his honor.

Philip Farkas, 1914-1992. He didn't play a second too long.

A chance to hear the trumpet float above the orchestra

I LIVED IN CHICAGO UNTIL I WAS eighteen and never heard of him, but when you grow up on the South Side, you never hear of a lot of famous people. After high school I attended Quincy College and majored in music but spent most of my time hanging out with a fifty-year-old French horn instructor who despised the 20th century.

"Stravinsky is a fraud," he'd say. "And so is James Joyce." His most frequent utterance was, "Hemingway should have been shot."

"He was shot," I'd remind him. "He blasted himself with a 12-gauge." This offered my mentor little comfort.

Anyway, the one person living in this century whom he felt should go on living in this century was the Chicago Symphony's principal trumpet player, Adolph Herseth. "Herseth," he'd say, "is the best damn trumpet player in the world."

Halfway through my sophomore year, the Chicago Symphony visited Quincy, Illinois. I can't remember much about the program except they played the Sibelius Second Symphony. Hearing Herseth that evening in a midwestern high school auditorium changed my life. "This is what I want to do for a living," I told the chairman of the music department.

"What?" he asked.

"Play like Herseth," I informed.

"But you play the trombone," he said.

"OK, I want to play like Herseth an octave lower."

I quit school, moved back to the family's South Side estate and began studying with a trombone player in the Chicago Symphony. On the wall of his studio were two pictures: one of his dog, the other of Herseth. At every lesson he'd point to the Herseth picture. "There's the guy we all try to sound like," he'd say.

In those years the symphony would give free tickets to Friday afternoon concerts to aspiring young players. I attended every one from September 1965 through June 1967. Herseth never disappointed me. "He was unbelievable this afternoon," I'd tell my mother over supper.

"What are you going to do for a living?" she would always ask, as if I should concern myself with such things at that point in my life.

But fate smiled on me. I completed a bachelor of music degree at the Chicago Conservatory and was hired by a college in Arkansas to teach trombone.

The trumpet teacher there owned every Chicago Symphony recording on which Herseth played. "Listen to how open his sound is on this one," he'd say as he put on the Hovhaness "Mysterious Mountain." "He floats above the whole orchestra."

A year later I did a little floating myself. To avoid dealing with Johnny Rambo I enlisted in the Navy music program. When I was assigned to a band in the North Atlantic, the chief petty officer interviewed me. "From Chicago, huh Zimmerman?"

"Yeah."

"Ever hear this guy Herseth play?"

"Every Friday afternoon for a couple of years."

"What size mouthpiece does he use to get a sound like that?"

"A big one," I said.

Three months later we played a concert in Helsinki, Finland. A musician from the Finnish National Radio Orchestra took me out for a few drinks afterward. "How does that Herseth do it?" he asked.

"Do what?"

"Play with that sound and float above the whole orchestra?"

"I wish I knew," I said. The amazing thing is that he's still doing it. He's the best damn trumpet player in the world.

TWELVE YEARS AGO THIS month Elvis bought the farm. Normally I don't notice such things, but I picked up Sunday's Trib and there on the first page of the Tempo section Bob Greene had produced still another Elvis column. In this one he marks the twelfth anniversary of the King's death by sleeping in Elvis' Las Vegas hotel suite.

Elvis, in case you don't remember, was a large Southern boy who once appeared on the Ed Sullivan show. Elvis later died, sending numerous Caucasians into a deep funk, which seems to recur every year at this time.

But hey, to each his own. I no longer feel that anyone who listens to rock music should be sent to a cultural re-education center or be subjected to bizarre medical experiments. Tolerance is my operative word these days. As a sensitive, caring guy preparing for the nineties, I no longer pass judgment on other types of music. And that's exactly why I took in a concert Saturday night that featured those darlings of the local new-age scene, Chicago's own Mannheim Steamroller.

For those unfamiliar with new-age music, suffice it to say that it is an attempt by major recording studios to heighten profits by taking old Montovani albums, adding the sound of gently falling rain or mating whales, then reissuing the album as something touched by the hand of Shirley MacLaine.

This stuff is just the ticket for today's yups and dinks who, after a day of trading commodities, like to put their feet up on the nearest ottoman or illegal alien and reconcile their yins and yangs, or at least their checkbooks.

The concert started with one of the Steamrollers conducting the accompanying symphony orchestra through a section of Respighi's "Pines of Rome." Naturally, that was the part of the piece that included birdcalls. The woman sitting next to me, a new-ager in her mid-thirties whose biodegradable clock was noticeably ticking, really got into it.

"Yeah!" she enthused. "It's happening tonight."

"The theme of tonight's program is nature," the announcer intoned. After a few selections from the standard classical nature repertoire, the Steamrollers performed their original nature repertoire, which utilized a gaggle of synthesizers, equalizers and numerous electronic gewgaws certain to quicken the pulse of attending new-agers and anyone else who enjoys looking at wallpaper catalogs.

Toward the end of the second half, in a reasonable facsimile of a tag team wrestling match, the Steamroller who had been conducting leaped from the podium, threw off his tuxedo jacket and began performing a paradiddle or two on the nearest conveniently located drumset.

Without missing a beat or a paradiddle, another Steamroller replaced him on the podium. Although equally enthused, Steamroller No. 2 kept his tuxedo on.

The crowd went wild at this bit of spontaneity. "Now it's really happening," gloated the woman next to me. She emphasized "really" as if there was a major step between "happening" and "really happening."

"Yeah," I said. "I just hope nobody gets hurt."

As the final piece ended, the crowd, fueled by enthusiasm, wine coolers and herbal tea, rose to its feet, giving the musicians a standing ovation.

"I guess it is really happening," I said.

Homage to a high school band director

VERNE REIMER WAS SO GOOD at directing a high school band that he was famous for it. He was the band director at York High School from 1951 until his retirement in 1976. If you mentioned his name to his contemporaries in California or New York, they would know of whom you were speaking. He was that famous. His was a different era.

Through the fifties and sixties this country was not the sports culture it is today. School sports for girls were almost non-existent, and a lot of kids were satisfied with one extracurricular activity, namely band. Overscheduling was not yet a way of life for us.

Schools were different then, too. If a teacher did a good job, he or she was left alone. Reimer did such a good job that he became an institution unto himself. Things aren't that way anymore.

Reimer's method of teaching wasn't unusual. He loved music and wanted to hear it played right. He told kids the truth. Some of them loved him for it, others didn't, but they all respected him.

Many of Reimer's college classmates became college and university band directors. Reimer could have done that. At the height of his career, he could have had his pick of college jobs. But he didn't want to; he just wanted to be a high school band director.

During the summer Reimer conducted the Wheaton Municipal Band. That's how I met him. Shortly before he retired and moved to California I spent two Sunday afternoons with him listening to auditions.

"Pshew," he said after a trombone player's audition. "Don't they teach counting anymore? I don't want that guy in my band." Reimer was tough. He wanted the right note at the right time and settled for nothing less. "Pshew! That sonovabitch sounds like he's moving furniture," he said after the departure of a tuba player who became hopelessly lost in the music.

I didn't realize that those were Reimerisms, and that they were recorded and collected over the years. It was a tradition in the York High School Band that after each rehearsal the first flute player wrote down every peculiar saying uttered by Reimer.

Mary Stolper of Elmhurst, first flute player in the York band from 1967-'71 and presently a professional flutist, presented me with four sets of Reimerisms. I'll quote a few:

"I sounded better sucking on straws at Sandy's"

"This one's going to be rough; it involves drummers."

"It's almost to the point of using foul language."

"The girl in the brown dress, can't you march without sticking out your butt?"

"What are you doing, working on a diploma in stupidity?"

"You have no audience presence. You walk in like you're going to feed the hogs or milk the cows."

"For the first time in my life I had to tune a saxophone."

"Studebaker can outblow the whole cornet section without trying."

The Studebaker he referred to was Julie Studebaker, first horn in the York band. She is now principal French horn in the Concertgebouw Orchestra of Holland and can still outblow whole cornet sections.

Reimer is here now for a while. Tomorrow former members of the York High School Band will gather and pay tribute to him, exchanging Reimerisms and recalling great and good moments together while visiting with the central figure of their youth.

I wish I were one of them.

Free concerts could become a thing of the past

IT WAS ONE OF THE BETTER breaks in a dismal musical career. On my third day of employment as a jogger in a print shop, Rocco the tuba player rescued me from a life of paper cuts by asking me to play trombone in his brass quintet.

The group was pretty good. Rocco had compiled an extensive library and from mid-September through June we'd play grade school concerts two or three times a week in the Chicago public schools.

We'd begin each concert by playing something loud and fast, hoping to impress the kids. After the final note of the first piece, Rocco would stand up and in his best music-educator voice say, "Good morning boys and girls. These are all brass instruments. This morning we'll show you how they work and what they sound like."

We'd play a few tunes and between selections each member would demonstrate his instrument. "This is a trombone," I would say, somewhat like Mr. Rogers introducing the concept of global warming. "It is the only brass instrument that doesn't have valves. Instead it has a slide to change the pitches of the notes." I'd then play the famous Dorsey solo, "I'm getting Sentimental Over You," which was pretty stupid now that I think about it; none of the kids knew who Dorsey was and most of the teachers didn't either.

After the final number the quintet members would sign a "green sheet" from the Music Performance Trust Fund, and in a couple of weeks each of us would receive a check for $35. Basically the schools raised half the money for a concert; the trust fund provided the other half by imposing a tariff of one-tenth of one percent on every record, CD and cassette tape sold in the U.S. Thanks to the trust fund, 35,000 free concerts are presented annually throughout the United States.

Rocco's quintet reached the zenith of its green-sheet career during the spring of 1973. He called me late one night. "We got the big one. A guy in Cleveland wants us to go there and play three school concerts and a formal evening concert! They're all trust fund so we know we'll get our money," he said.

"Wait a minute, Rocco." I said. "We get 35 bucks apiece for trust fund concerts. Is it worth it to drive to Cleveland for $140?"

"I've saved the best part for last," Rocco gushed. "The guy is going to slip us an extra twenty bucks apiece under the table. How can we go wrong?"

A used set of tails for the formal evening concert cost me $35. Rocco, who at the time tipped in at around 320 pounds, wasn't as lucky.

The Cleveland school concerts went without a hitch, but the audience for the formal evening concert consisted of four people, one of whom was my wife.

"Jeez," Rocco said. "We could have skipped buying tails and played in our tuxes."

The Ohio impresario stiffed us on the under-the-table money, but three weeks later the Musicians Performance Trust Fund sent us each four checks for 35 bucks.

Struggling musicians of the future may not have the trust fund to fall back on. Talks between the American Federation of Musicians and the record industry begin next week. Many of the record companies that control the American market are now foreign-owned and want no part of subsidizing U.S. culture, even if it costs them only a little more than a penny on every record, tape or CD.

That's too bad. Summer band concerts in the park and free performances in old folks' homes and veterans hospitals could become a thing of the past.

So could guys like Rocco and me.

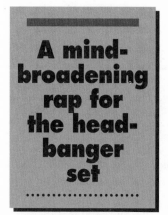

A mind-broadening rap for the head-banger set

MY KID AND HIS FRIENDS listen to rap and heavy-metal music. Rap features inner-city types who rhyme socially significant messages.

"Dee man is white and thinks he's cool/But he ain't no brother so he's a fool" (repeated 237 times while accompanied by a bad rhythm section).

If you watch rap videos you will notice that most rappers deliver their messages while making grotesque gestures with their hands and fingers, much like the Hunchback of Notre Dame dialing a telephone. I don't know what the significance of this is.

Heavy-metal music consists of leather-clad youth with incredibly long hair who play electronic instruments developed by the KGB's interrogation division. In college I had a professor who liked to show that art doesn't just happen. He often asked the age-old question: "If you gave a million monkeys typewriters, how long would it be before they produced *Paradise Lost?*" Probably never, especially without spell-check.

But give four chimps a couple of guitars, some Marshall amps and a drum set, and they should be able to knock out a heavy-metal hit within four to seven minutes. There is one other aspect of this art form: head banging. When a heavy-metal rocker really gets into it, he starts slamming his head up and down, and within seconds, so does his audience.

I've taken a verse from Metallica's *Master of Puppets* album and indicated the appropriate places for head bangs, just in case you find yourself in a room full of heavy-metal types and want to fit in.

Master of Puppets I'm pulling your strings (bang!)
Twisting your mind and smashing your dreams (bang!)
Blinded by me (Bang!), you can't see a thing (Bang! Bang!)

Just call my name (Bang!) cause I'll hear you scream (BANG! BANG! BANG! BANG!).

My kid has complained of a stiff neck after attending heavy-metal concerts. One good thing, though: if he masters head-banging and those grotesque rapper hand signals, no draft board will ever touch him.

Anyway, I've come up with a little scheme to broaden the horizons of rappers and heavy-metal freaks. Thus, I am offering rappers and heavy metallurgists a chance to break free without the help of Thorazine or a twelve-step recovery program. The 25th Elmhurst College Jazz Festival takes place the weekend of February 28-March 1 at the college's Hammerschmidt Chapel. There, talented young musicians will perform without offering socially significant rhymes, weird hand signals or head-banging. But more bizarre than that, all the drummers who appear that weekend will wear shirts!

If you are into rap or heavy metal and would like to hear a jazz concert, or at least see a drummer wearing a shirt, meet me on the steps of Hammerschmidt Chapel before the 1 p.m. Saturday session of the Elmhurst College Jazz Festival. Bring me any rap or heavy-metal compact disc and I will see that you get in free.

The cost of your ticket is not coming out of my pocket, however. The festival's producer and Numero Uno jazz fan, James Cunningham, has agreed to this as a way to attract new listeners to America's original musical art form.

It's not a bad deal. Just don't ask for the CD back. Cunningham and I are avid skeet shooters.

Memories of earliest solos linger long after notes ebb

IT'S A LITTLE BIT OF AMERICANA of which most are unaware. Every year at this time kids who play in a school band or orchestra get ready for a solo and ensemble contest. But they aren't called contests anymore; kids really don't compete against one another as they once did. Instead they play before a judge, who fills out a comment sheet and assigns each player a number that seems to stay with the kid forever, or at least until summer vacation.

"I got a one!" kids who play well brag. Those with fours usually say nothing, but mope for a day or two before rationalizing away the experience. "The judge didn't give me time to get used to the room," they say.

In my dreams I see the number "two" followed by "Needs a little more preparation," on my sophomore year's comment sheet. And I still see the big "one" followed by "Bravo!" written on the sheet of a little twerp who never practiced and who could never play the trombone as well as I did, even on his best day. That was thirty years ago and it's still with me.

Kids are usually assigned solos after Christmas, which means they practice them minimally for a while, then in a flurry of private lessons, get very serious late in February.

Judges are very serious too. Except they are called adjudicators, God knows why. For not a lot of money, they sit in a classroom all day listening to kids, some good, some bad, play solos titled "Garnet" or "Topaz" with piano accompaniment. Or they hear kids huff and puff their way through duets, trios and quartets that have names like "Chorale from Dvorak's New World Symphony Arranged for Brass Quartet."

"Tommy, good job! But you should work more on rhythm. Try to get all your dotted-eighth-and-sixteenths consistent," they scrawl every five minutes for eight hours.

Most adjudicators are themselves music teachers from different school districts. For an entire Saturday of my young adult life I judged high school kids for a music contest in Little Rock, Arkansas. I was asked to rate the players in order of their ability, which in turn determined who got into the Arkansas All-State band and who didn't. People in Arkansas take this stuff very seriously.

I picked the worst kid possible as the best trombone player in the state. What can I say? I added up all the numbers in all the categories and Billy Bob something or other came out on top.

Billy Bob was known throughout Arkansas as a major goof-off, and when his name was announced people asked if it were a joke.

I wish it were. Billy Bob was so despised that his band director buttonholed me and, in a scene similar to "What we have here is a failure to communicate" from *Cool Hand Luke,* summed up my musical knowledge in a single sentence that used the word Shineola. I wasn't asked back.

Presently, my thirteen-year-old son is preparing his solo for next month's outing. Each night he plays through it several times. "Stay in tempo," I constantly yell from the next room. "Find a different reed," his mother says. "That one is too soft."

As his moment approaches he spends as much time with his clarinet as he spends in the shower. There will be a few more rehearsals and then early on a Saturday morning his mother and I will drive him to a nearby school. Sitting nervously in the back, we'll listen to him and the accompanist play through the solo for the adjudicator. The whole thing takes less than five minutes, yet I can remember every one of my trips to solo contest and what it felt like standing up there all alone, just me, the instrument and some music.

It's an education, a moment of truth. Some kids who prepare diligently will blow it, other kids might play way above their level the way Billy Bob did. But for most, the amount of preparation equals the level of performance. Few of these kids go on to earn a living in music. It doesn't matter, though. Once or twice in life everybody has to stand up there all alone.

■

9

HUH?

Is it Michael, or is it just another tall guy in short pants?

HEY, LIGHTEN UP EVERY-BODY, he's only a basketball player. Every time I turn around some awestruck ninny is prostrating himself at the guy's feet. Look, Michael Jordan is a wonderful guy, a sterling example to our youth, the greatest player to have lived or to have played the game or whatever sportswriters are saying these days. But it's only basketball, a game for tall men in short pants.

After the final in the series with Detroit, Chet Whoosits came on the radio and pondered, "Just how long can this young man be denied a championship ring?" It was touching, and I'm sure that Jordan fans everywhere along with the Chetster shook their heads from side to side while lumps formed in their throats as they contemplated the immensity of this tragedy.

I hate to inform them that if Michael stays with the Bulls and the Bulls never win a championship (let's see, if A = B and B = C, then C must = A), then Michael will never win a championship ring!

Yeah, I know it is a great injustice, right up there with Solzhenitsyn freezing his butt off in a Siberian gulag or Steve Biko getting his guts kicked out by the South African police, but after all, isn't sports supposed to be a metaphor for life? Besides, Jordan is only twenty-seven years old and owns three cars, none of which is jacked up in his front yard with concrete blocks under its axles; just how tough can things be?

Bob Greene, famous Tribune columnist and Elvis historian, informed his readership in last Sunday's column that "Jordan has become that rare individual who, when he walks into a room, literally brings tears to people's eyes." Christ didn't receive this much adulation in his lifetime, but then He didn't endorse athletic shoes that went for $130 a pair.

Unfortunately, I have some bad news for Michael Jordan fans. Once I disclose this my days will be numbered, but such is the high price of suburban journalism.

You see, Michael Jordan doesn't really exist. Yeah, I know you've seen him on TV and maybe even in person, but that's an actor from the Cosby Show who plays Michael Jordan. It's sort of like Betty Crocker, a figment of corporate America's imagination, manufactured solely for product endorsement.

What they do is videotape this guy in a Bulls uniform leaping around a basketball court, slam-dunking or sailing over the heads of a couple of defenders who are also paid actors. But they do this before the game. Then when Michael executes a similar play in the real game, one of the engineers at the station electronically splices in the pre-game shenanigans.

If you look real close at some of those plays, you'll see the edge of a tiny trampoline that Jordan uses to get all that hang time. Of course, the people at the stadium don't see the same Michael that the people at home see, but they are victims of crowd hysteria or too much MSG in their egg rolls or something.

Later when they watch the replays on the evening news, they are faced with either believing what they saw in person a few hours before or what they are seeing now on a news broadcast.

Typical of avid sports fans, they have more faith in their TV sets.

Don't count sheep; Just grab TV remote

MIDNIGHT. CAN'T SLEEP. Murphy Brown's kid. No father to drive him to soccer. Will he know the difference between rip and crosscut saws? Forget him. Got my own problems. Try TV.

Monitor Channel. Four severe women talk about unwed welfare mothers. Commercial. Thin woman in bathing suit lolls on the California coastline. Listening to a Sony Walkman. Selling Sony Walkmans? No! four-record set *Everlasting Love*. Send $19.95 to Omaha, Neb. Omaha? Nobody owns a bathing suit in Omaha. Nobody owns records in Omaha.

Check out Channel 48. Uh-oh, book on home remedies. "Use hair dryer to cure ear aches. Rub aspirin on a bee sting." Got my own home remedy. Tape VISA card to upper arm like nicotine patch. Haven't charged anything in weeks.

Wait a minute. Channel 48 is "The International Channel." They're speaking Chinese with Korean subtitles. Nose flute and amplified cheese cutter provide background music.

Change channel. CNN. "Potential running mates for Bill Clinton and Ross Perot?" Who cares? Lyndon LaRouche's my man. Commercial. Remote Hide-Away. Place to store your TV remote. It looks like a book. But it's hollow and sells for $29.95! That's stupid. Make mental note: Buy copy of *The Rise and Fall of the Third Reich* at used bookstore. Cut out pages 26 through 659 and keep remote inside. Zimm, how do you do it?

Paid programming. Channel 66. Half an hour of Acne-Statin acne medication. One testimonial after another. "I'm dating several girls right now." "You can go out of the house and smile at people again." "To a teen-ager, complexion problems can be a matter of life and death." Uh-oh hidden message—buy this stuff or your teen-ager might play Dungeons and Dragons inside heating ducts. Dr. Atida Karr, inventor of Acne-Statin: "I'm not a miracle worker—I'm a physician," she says.

Cut to more personal experiences. "I lost a year of my life to acne." Good on diaper rash, too. "I was on a trip and my baby..." Mental note: Get some for long bike trips.

Change channel. Channel 32. "Psychic Friends Network." Dionne Warwick is host. Must be having bad times. Linda Georgian, middle-aged psychic earth mother: "Your call can be automatically channeled to the home or office of an approved psychic."

Re-enactment: "The brakeline was leaking. The car will crash in minutes," phone-psychic Bonita told Dawn. Dawn grabs Shadell in parking lot just as she was about to pull away. Chalk up another life saved for the Psychic Friends Network, where everybody talks in simple sentences. "Call a psychic friend now!" 1-900 number. Small print says $3.99 a minute. Cut to commercial. Not real commercial because whole show is a commercial.

Fisherman: "The best fishing trip we ever had, all because of Psychic Friends Network." Friend agrees, then snorts.

Back to Dionne and Linda at the studio. Last words of show: "Our psychics are standing by!"

Change to Channel 10. More paid programming. Robert Tilton Ministry. He flaps for a while, thumps a zippered Bible and screws up his face. Cut to dramatized vignette. Sam is out of work and has furniture just like mine. I'm depressed. Sam pledges 500 bucks to the Robert Tilton ministry. Does he have it? Naw. But a few days later Sam gets dream job—sixty big ones! Announcer: "Every day is a steak-and-potatoes day!"

Mental note: Find some guys as dumb as Sam and retire for life.

Search for 12-inch tires drives grown man to fantasize

I T STARTED SIMPLY ENOUGH: my car needed two front tires. It wasn't a big deal in the grand scheme of things. People buy tires every day. But my car is a subcompact, which means it was built overseas in a factory where workers do morning calisthenics before screwing on the day's first lug nut. It also means the car was equipped with 12-inch tires, these from a country where parents bound their daughters' feet.

I went to a couple of places, watched the clerks scratch their heads and snort as they called their buddies at other tire stores to locate a pair of 12-inch radials. No luck. "Buy a new car," the wife said when I came home with the same front tires I left with.

"Can't afford it," I said.

She was not deterred by reality. "Get something nice with air conditioning. Maybe you should buy a used BMW." Quite a jump considering my car has rear windows that don't roll down. But I have fantasized about owning one of those cute little $30,000 jobs built by the same people who gave us Bavarian creme tortes, beer hall putsches and Adolf Hitler.

"You'll think about buying a BMW for a while but you won't. You always talk about stuff that you never do," the youngest mouth-breather lectured.

"I'm a writer. I live in my mind where it is cheaper," I told him. "I'm almost forty-six and driving a car with manual transmission and no air conditioning. But it doesn't bother me." Still, though, the thought of tooling around in a BMW seemed pretty appealing.

The years had been kind to Jack. He could now reflect on his past several decades with a sense of satisfaction as he drove the BMW to pick up his third Pulitzer. With his tan arm protruding from the window and his shock of salt-and-pepper hair dancing in the breeze, he felt that life had smiled upon him. "Writing has been very good to me," he thought as he navigated another hairpin turn at 95 miles an hour...

My kids liked the idea of a BMW in our driveway. My oldest son confided that his friends refer to my present car as "the golf cart."

"People wait five years for a car like that in Soviet Bloc countries," I said, but this did little to console him.

"What about an Acura?" my youngest asked.

"They look like something an accountant drives," I told him. But there have been times I've thought of owning one.

The white Acura coupe knifed through the early evening Loop traffic. For most it would be the honor of a lifetime, but for him it was just another Man of the Year Award. "Damn," he thought. "I'll have to sign autographs after the photo session." His unfinished novel awaited his return home, but he wasn't troubled by this. He had thirteen published works to his credit; ten eventually became movies. "How do you do it, Jack?" were the words most often uttered by his adoring public...

The following morning I found a pair of 12-inch tires on sale for 23 bucks apiece. All speculation on BMWs and Acuras ceased. After investing this kind of money, I plan to keep my present vehicle until it flunks an emission test.

She caught his glance as she pulled alongside him on the interstate. Despite her career as an actress and model and her dozens of suitors, there was something about this man that was so appealing. "He's probably the same age as my father," she thought. "But he's so at ease with himself that he drives a Ford Festiva without air conditioning. I just wish I could be alone with him..."

**Urbane
fantasies
expire from
excess
cultivation**

OR MOST OF MY ADULT LIFE I was a city person who lived in the suburbs. Even though I owned a home in DuPage County for sixteen years, I fantasized about the day my youngest would leave for college. Then my wife and I would move into a Near North loft furnished with director's chairs, platform beds and one of those dopey Italian reading lamps that looks like an oversized parakeet toy. In this fantasy I'm a thin, published novelist who sips tall cool ones in the afternoon with Saul Bellow or at least Bill Granger. But my fantasy recently died. It was killed by two trips into the city.

The gallery openings There's no better way to eat and drink for free than to attend gallery openings. Basically, an artist paints twenty or thirty pictures, hangs them in a gallery located in a blighted neighborhood, buys four gallon bottles of Gallo wine, several packages of Kraft Sliced Singles and invites pointy-headed intellectoids, bicycle messengers and women who don't wear makeup. Last Friday I attended three openings. Being the only male without an earring or work boots didn't bother me. One of the galleries was full of men my father would have punched in the mouth for the way they dressed. Conversations were much the same in all three openings.

> Gallery attendee No. 1: I've noticed a change in his work. He's not using body parts anymore.
> Gallery attendee No. 2: I thought so at first, but if you look closer there are eyeballs there. He hasn't completely broken with the past.
> Gallery attendee No. 1: But he has taken an important step.
> Gallery attendee No. 2: Yes, but kinetic realism isn't a country you visit occasionally.

After a while I got a headache from looking at pictures drawn by guys who just took important steps.

The last opening I went to on Friday featured eyeglass frames fastened to a bicycle wheel. As the wheel revolved, the frames were dragged through a puddle of soap solution and then an electric fan blew bubbles from them. I was glad to get home.

The signing A woman I worked with called to tell me that her college English instructor, The Great Southern Writer, would be in town signing copies of his latest literary effort. He appeared at a bookstore on North Broadway where he read one of his short stories. Sixty people who looked as if they lived in Printers Row and listened to too much National Public Radio showed up and doted and clucked over his every metaphor. After the short story, the rest of the evening was devoted to a question-and-answer session.

Adoring reader: What do you think of the coming presidential election?

The Great Southern Writer: As a great Southern writer I just want to say that all Southern writers are great (applause) because we lost the war and have had time to reflect (more applause). As you know, I don't own a television (applause) but I call wonderful friends all over the country (applause) and in my fiction I try to reconcile the horrible characters that populate the headlines with the wonderful friends I have in my address book (thunderous applause).

Adoring reader: O Great Southern Writer, we think you're wonderful (foot stomping and bravos)!

I realized then that if I moved to the city, these adoring readers would be my neighbors. This is frightening.

Don't forget to use the joke about the chicken and the pig

M AN, THIS NEW CALLER ID IS great. Uh-oh, let that one ring. 800 numbers mean trouble. Probably forgot to make that last VISA payment. The way this thing works is simple. As soon as the phone rings this little gizmo gives me the number of the caller. Hey, that's my mother's number. "Hello, Mother."

"How did you know it was me?"

"We've always had a certain closeness."

"Don't give me that. How did you know?"

"Actually, I've been practicing this mental stuff. I willed you to call."

"If that's the case, I'll call you again sometime when it is my idea. Goodbye."

Keep a log book near the telephone, and when you get a jerky call from an unknown number, write it down so the next time you can take a pass on answering it.

"Mr. Zimmerman?"

"Yeah."

"How you doin' tonight?"

"I'm in the middle of one of the best meals I've ever eaten."

"This will only take a minute. As you know summer is the time for home improvements, and we have several trucks in your area this week."

"What's the point?"

"Gutters and downspouts, screened-in porches, dog runs."

"Yeah, we could use the works. I just came into a little inheritance and the wife and I want to..." It really gets them when you hang up in mid-sentence when the old juices are flowing. They think it is a technical problem. When they call back, try this one:

"ALLO."

"Mr. Zimmerman?"

"Non."

"Is Mr. Zimmerman there?" "Je ne parle pas Anglais." "Is this the Zimmerman household?" "Je ne parle pas Anglais."

All that time watching those Truffaut movies finally pays off. Isn't this more fun than a flat "no?" As far as crank calls from kids go, you can't beat this.

Consider the typical pre-adolescent midnight pizza party/sleep-over crank call. "Ummm. Is your refrigerator running?"

"Yeah, why?"

"You better catch it. Ha, ha, ha, ha."

With caller ID you can call the little grifter's parents the next morning as they're getting to sleep. "Why did the chicken cross the road?"

"I dunno."

"'Cause he was stapled to the pig. Ha, ha, ha, ha."

But wait. Some civil libertarian ninnies want to deprive us of all this. They say Caller ID violates the caller's constitutional right to privacy. People will be reluctant to call crisis hotlines. Battered women won't call home because Caller ID will give away their whereabouts. Tipsters will no longer make anonymous calls to the police because their phone numbers will be recorded. Husbands won't call their wives from the local gin mill to inform them that they're working late. Our whole society will unravel. Oprah will do a program about it.

There's an easy way around this, though. Say you're a battered wife who would like to call her lout of a husband, God knows why, or a concerned citizen who'd like to inform the local building inspector of an illegal sump pump connection, and you'd like to conceal your identity. Instead of calling from the shelter, use an outside public phone. It might be a little inconvenient, but it's worth the effort. And be sure to use the chicken-and-the-pig joke.

The forgotten quatrains

JAPAN AS THE WORLD'S NUMERO Uno economic power? The president of the United States blowing lunch? Lake Michigan water in DuPage County? These events may be strange to many, but I could have predicted them years ago. I'm no psychic. Until recently I didn't even believe in that stuff.

But through a weird set of circumstances, I own the only existing copy of Nostradamus' *The Other Quatrains*. I found the book in the dryer of an existentialist laundromat I frequented (the laundromat, not the dryer) during the 1960s. Nostradamus, a French liver-paté salesman and close friend of Orson Welles, liked to pen little bagatelles, which many swear predict the future. I was skeptical until I dug out my copy of *The Other Quatrains,* which I presently keep in my own dryer, and read No. 46.

> After the great war and conflagration, the vanquished will become the champions. The new war will not be fought with weapons of war but with weapons of peace. The prince of the West will meet the King of Factories and beg for mercy. After much discussion the King of Factories will show no mercy, so the Prince will ruin his carpet.

Just coincidence? Perhaps, but a close look at quatrain 62 shows that Nostradamus had more than liver pate and Glenn Close in a push-up bra on his mind.

> Those to the west of the City of Broadness will thirst—their water, the earth's bile. While those of the City of Broadness drink forever freely from the inland sea. But those of the city, their broadness diminishing, sell their precious sea water to those of the west, who soon grow to be like them and send their offspring to bad schools.

The thing that makes Nostradamus so appealing is that he

concerns himself with more than just economic and political issues. Take a gander at the 72nd quatrain.

> The great bear of the north will do much weeping and gnashing of teeth until his followers, the other bears of the north, withstand the assault of their enemies and the coldest of bears reduces his girth. Only when the great bear's weeping and gnashing stops will he regain his former product endorsements and splendor. Once more, Michael of the Ground will equal Michael of the Air in the eyes of those who worship him.

Titled "The Village That Works" Quatrain, his 98th predicted the conversion of Villa Park's Ovaltine factory to a home for old geezers.

> In the midst of the tiny village is a great edifice, once home of Annie of no parents. Saddened by its emptiness, those of power and influence, after six years of discussion, change the great structure to give succor to elders who drink hot chocolate and wear decoder rings.

Of course, some quatrains cannot be interpreted. For the last several weeks I've looked at the 23rd quatrain, but I can't figure it out, even though it seems strangely familiar.

> The bored are my leopards, I shall not taunt. They shake me down with green plaster and lead me beside shrill daughters.

Obviously, the guy was overcome by liver paté fumes or watched too much MTV the day he wrote that one.

This fashion plate has all the clothes that he'll ever need

I RARELY BUY NEW CLOTHES, AND I own only two pairs of pants. My blue polyesters with a white shirt give me the appearance of an off-duty Chicago policeman. My black polyesters worn with a short-sleeved plaid make me look like a Catholic priest on vacation.

Nonetheless, my house has been deluged with clothing catalogues of late. From where they got my name, God only knows, but thanks to direct-mail advertising I'm regularly visited by Eddie Bauer, Lands' End and a host of others. But I'm not complaining. They make for better reading than the Trib's Tempo Section. Instead of the usual single paragraph full of hyphenated modifiers like most catalogue copy, Lands' End offers a short story on each item. Take a gander at this sparkler: "Ah, the Gingham is even more welcome because, ahem, we do have a certain reputation. (You can count on a greater likelihood of 'oohs' and 'aahs' when they see the label. Trust us.)" The copy runs on for several more paragraphs before mentioning size or price. Unfortunately, Lands' End models look like genetic experiments conducted by Pat Boone and Sandy Duncan. Most of the women try for Midwestern chicness by wearing mid-calf cotton dresses—"Look closely at this new dress, and you'll see an etched pattern of wild roses and buds on twining vines..."; ragg socks —"Knit thick with ragg yarns so your feet stay warm, cushioned, blister-free..."; and shoes that are leftovers from a Stalin Five-Year Plan—"Our invincible Pac Boots are as tough as they come!"

Eddie Bauer's women aren't much different except that they frequently pose with horses while gazing at some far-off vista—twenty-five-year-old Becky Thatchers waiting for Tom and Huck to come home to the farm after a rough day in the commodity pits. While the women may seem interesting, Bauer's copy isn't. "Don't face winter without the protection of our Canvas/Down

Topper." Sounds like a condom ad. However, Bauer's catalogue offers occasional environmental tips: "Properly dispose of trash when fishing or boating; discarded fishing line and plastic rope kill wildlife." "Compost grass clippings and coarse vegetation in a ventilated bin to produce organic nutrients for the soil," is one of my favorites.

Bauer's men have that Martin Sheen I'm-a-sensitive-caring-guy-of-the-90s air, which sure beats all those shiny-chinned Nordic types from Lands' End. I'd buy stuff from either of these companies except that men's sizes run only to a skimpy 48, and my 40/30 waist-inseam ratio is off the charts. Besides, I've got all the clothes I'll ever need. Today I'm wearing the black polyesters and the short-sleeved plaid. Peace be with you.

When art is seen as the enemy, we lose

IT WAS THE OLD ART THAT eventually got Ziggy into trouble. I told him not to listen to it or look at it anymore, but he was one of those guys who was a sucker for beautiful things—a twentiethth-century man living in the twenty-fifth century. He often told me about the way things once were, how people would go to these places called museums and look at pictures that would make them feel different ways, sometimes sad, sometimes happy. The old art could make people really mad, too.

"It made them think. That was once an important part of being human," Ziggy said. I always agreed with him but only because I didn't want to argue. He also told me about concerts in the twentieth century. People would sit in a big room together and listen to other people perform on musical instruments. Those who wrote the music for these events were often considered geniuses. The performers studied their entire lives so they could interpret the works. Ziggy once talked about a concert in Paris in the early twentiethth century. A new work was played that was so revolutionary that a riot broke out. It seems ridiculous now that people would be that affected by combinations of sounds. I pointed this out to Ziggy. "At least they were alive and vibrant," he said. "But why would they want to have something that stirred up trouble like that?" Ziggy maintained that people got something special from going to museums and concert halls, and that the old art made people examine their lives and celebrate their humanness. I never understood any of this. But because I was his friend, I'd just nod in agreement.

The weirdest thing he told me about the twentieth century was that for a time, government actually paid artists to paint, write and compose. They must have been pretty stupid back then to do something as unproductive as that. Why would government encourage people who were different? And didn't they realize that

creativity was the enemy of efficiency? Luckily some of their elect-
ed representatives were smart enough to see the folly and coun-
terproductivity of this nonsense. They put a stop to it. Of course,
artists continued writing, painting and composing, but gradually
over the next several centuries these things became less and less
important to real folks. After all, studying art made people spend
time away from their work or watching the games.

Pretty soon artists themselves were looked upon as historical
curiosities. They lived in colonies that were tourist attractions. I
remember as a kid my family once stopped in one on a summer
vacation. The place was real weird because they had this thing
called architecture. Get this—buildings were supposed to be different from one another! We heard some recorded music there
and looked at paintings. None of it made any sense to us, and our
tour guide told us that it took a great deal of study and reflection
to understand the old art, and even at the time it was created people had differing views about it. Some liked it and others despised
it. But that was the neat thing, it made people think.

Anyway, Ziggy spent more and more of his time listening to
music written by composers and staring at books of the old paintings. After a while he stopped attending the games and his family
became concerned. At his sanity hearing he rambled on about
truth and beauty and the nobility of the human spirit and how we
had lost something. Just the fact that he showed so much passion
was enough to convict him. The judge ordered a cranial implant
unit. It must have worked because I see him at all the games now.

Scurrilous, shameless and (I hope) lucrative

ANOTHER UNAUTHORIZED biography hit the bookstore shelves this week. This time it's Ted Kennedy who is accused of snorting cocaine and romping in the sheets with women half his age. A few of Kennedy's close associates have gone on television to say the book contains half-truths, non-truths, and outright lies. According to sources, Kennedy is considering a libel suit against the author, a one-time staffer who filed for bankruptcy last year and who once staged a phony assassination attempt on himself.

Despite its inaccuracies, the book will probably sell a few million copies. Unauthorized biographies are this country's favorite literary form. Kennedy will reap a ton of publicity from media interviews where he'll utter, "completely untrue, nothing but scurrilous accusations and shameless character assassination."

As Tony Fitzpatrick, Villa Park's No. 1 media manipulator, often said, "Bad PR beats no PR."

It's true. Try to name Massachusetts' other senator. Despite a lifetime of boozy parties and late-night trips to police stations, Ted Kennedy is more famous than anyone else in Congress.

But why should he have all this fame? He's got a job with a regular paycheck, drives an air-conditioned car and has several million stashed in a trust set up by his old man. He doesn't need fame.

But I do. I'm tired of driving a Festiva and going to parties with other middle-aged guys who wear sweaters with sailboats on them and who talk about bypass surgery and retirement annuities.

Nobody is going to write a book about me, libelous or otherwise. Thus, I've developed a new literary form—the unauthorized autobiography. Here's a sample chapter:

> It was getting late and she slipped the Taurus into drive as we left the summer house in Brandywine. I could still hear the

others at the party. That game of Uno had become pretty wild.

"How do you do it, Jack?" she asked as she held her lips in a fake pout.

"I don't know," I told her. "I guess it's talent."

I reached into the glove compartment and poured us both a shot of Ovaltine from the thermos. It felt good going down and made her shudder. She put her hand on my knee and her nostrils quivered. Even though she was twenty-six years older than me, there was that certain attraction.

"Do you have protection?" I asked, knowing full well where the evening was headed.

"Wouldn't be without it," she purred. "I've had an AARP Supplemental Health Plan for years. Medicare can't cover everything."

She was right. I let her drop me at home. "Will I ever see you again?" she asked.

"Of course you will," I lied, knowing that in the morning I'd be leaving for the Orkin training program while she would have hip replacement surgery. She's just after my money, I thought.

She knew I was lying and jammed her Enna Jettick down on the gas pedal. "You men are such bastards," she screamed.

Those real estate people are all alike, I thought. Give them a listing and they think they own you. I wasn't going to redecorate no matter what she said. Yeah, I wanted to sell the place, but not if it meant getting rid of everything I worked for. "What's so bad about orange shag?" I yelled, but she couldn't hear me. The taillights of the Taurus slowly disappeared into the night...

Of course, it needs a little more work. With a few torrid sex scenes involving a midget insurance adjustor, I'll have a best-seller. And then I'll appear on talk shows saying, "Completely untrue, nothing but scurrilous accusations and shameless character assassination."

Great expectorations, but net effect was rinky-dink

"YOU HAVE TO GO," HE said. "It will be a new experience for you. Besides, the seats cost $60 apiece. A guy gave them to me." I don't go to sporting events because I hate all sports. Bad experience in my high school locker room. Sharing these things with him did little good, though.

"Ever been to a professional hockey game?"

I told him no, that I abhor violence, that I can't even watch the Three Stooges, that I haven't eaten meat in three years, that I'm a very private person who requires his own washroom facilities. He didn't give up. Sports people are that way, true believers.

"You might learn something new, and you have to hear them do the national anthem at the Stadium. Everybody screams through the whole thing. It's a Chicago tradition, like not doing the wave at Wrigley Field." He once made me sit through an Arena Football game at the Rosemont Horizon. He has that kind of power over me. "How do you know you don't like something unless you try it?" This guy doesn't stop. I considered using the old I've-never-been-hit-by-a-car-but-I'm-sure-I-wouldn't-like-it argument, but weakened instead.

We paid $8 to park. It's only $4.50 at Chicago Symphony concerts, but there you don't get to see grown men bleed on one another unless the orchestra is playing Bruckner and Solti is in town.

"Will there be cars parked directly behind us, or will we be able to get out if we leave early?" the sports missionary asked.

"Can't get out (spit). If you wanna get out (snort), those spaces are $10 (spit, snort, spit, snort)," the attendant, played by a young Walter Brennan, explained.

We took the $8 spot. Our seats were directly behind the goal. The pucks hit the transparent shield a few feet in front of us with a frightening WHACK! as the players practiced shots. Sixty bucks for this, I thought; my seat at the opera is only 30. The Zamboni made a few passes as it resurfaced the ice. Do Zamboni drivers have other jobs? Is there such a thing as a free-lance Zamboni driver, a guy who sits at home waiting for the big break? Has anyone ever fallen off a Zamboni? Anybody killed in a Zamboni accident? These thoughts were very troubling.

A beautiful woman sat beside me. Huge diamond ring. Huge diamond earrings. Huge... She chewed gum and talked to another beautiful woman with matching jewelry. They spoke with heavy Chicago accents—worse than mine—and ended every sentence with a preposition. "Where you going to?" "I don't know where it's at," they said.

They didn't get who or whom straight either. I was about to give them my free lecture on objective case, but everybody began screaming for the national anthem.

The women's dates arrived—two guys with leather overcoats, a lot of testosterone and Cro-Magnon-shaped skulls.

"How's about that Eddie?" one Cro-Magnon asked me. I told him that Eddie was very smooth, hoping he wouldn't realize this was my first hockey game ever and I didn't know or care who the hell Eddie was.

The Cro-Magnon looked like one of those football players who teased me in my high school locker room. I was afraid he'd do it again, but Eddie being smooth satisfied him.

"Yeah, he's smooth all right," he said, squinting as if looking at the horizon while he chipped a stone into the shape of an arrowhead.

Another troubling thought—Do hockey pucks wear out? I wanted to ask someone but was afraid of a lengthy explanation.

After three periods of professional hockey and making small talk to the Cro-Magnons and the Cro-Magnonettes, we headed home. "Thanks for coming," the sports missionary said as I dropped him at his house.

"Thanks for asking me," I said. "And I did learn something new — spit, snort, spit, snort."

DuPage courts tradition of monumental failures

M OST DAYS I'M DEPRESSED. It's not a big deal, just the way I look at life. Some people say the glass is half-empty, others say it is half-full. I worry about washing it when those idiots are done with their stupid philosophical discussions.

But even though I'm good at being depressed, I like to take a breather once in a while and look at the bright side of life, as if I were born into a family of Amway distributors or Ross Perot supporters.

Becoming a positive type is not easy. Most people elevate their moods by reading an uplifting book like *Jonathan Livingston Seagull,* watching *The Sound of Music* or listening to a motivational tape that tells them they are really someone important and deserving of love and respect from their fellow...blah, blah, blah...

This stuff doesn't do anything for me. Show me a self-help book full of it's-the-journey-not-the-destination drivel, and I'm ready to check into the nearest depressive disorders clinic. But given an example of colossal failure, of good intentions gone wrong, and my spirits are lifted; I become almost euphoric.

The problem is that failure, like success, can be fleeting. Who still thinks about *Heaven's Gate,* Hollywood's most expensive failure of all time? Or how often does anyone reflect on the hundreds of TV programs that lasted a few episodes and were dumped because of low ratings?

Nobody thinks of these things anymore because they are no longer here. That's the way most failures are. For a time they are talked about, but then forgotten. The 1984 Mondale campaign just doesn't do it for me.

Architectural failures are different, though. Put up a building that's a loser and people will look at it daily for at least half a century. Unlike presidential campaigns, failures in architecture just don't go away. Consider the Loop's State of Illinois Building. No matter how depressed I might be, a walk through the butt-ugly lobby of this thing brightens my day. Here is the product of a major architect, a multi-term governor of one of this nation's most populous states, and this is what they came up with—a building that resembles the Rotor at Riverview. Millions of dollars, some of the best minds with some of the best intentions, and we are left with an expensive public building made of the same materials used in mobile homes. Luckily, though, I no longer have to commute into the city to have my day brightened by public building design flaws.

DuPage County, long famous for public buildings that spit bricks, now offers a courthouse rich in the jeez-I-dunno-what's-wrong-tradition. Fifty-three-million bucks and it accomplishes the same thing as spoiled tuna salad; it makes people sick.

I love it. And I love thinking about all the architects, engineers, building inspectors and political coatholders who got a piece of that $53 million. They're all competent, honorable and dedicated. But not one of them looked at this thing and said, "Hey, for $53 million we ought to put in old-fashioned windows that employees can open in case they need fresh air and maybe toss in a couple of ceiling fans that are on sale at Builders Square."

But that is life in DuPage. Our failures are as good as anybody's.

How to drive your favorite soap opera fans into a lather

EVER NOTICE THAT PEOPLE who have less than a brain are usually big soap opera fans? Let's face it, if they didn't have the soaps, they'd spend all their time answering chain letters, sending money to televangelists or buying cats that have clocks in their stomachs.

More bizarre: There's a column in the Saturday Tribune called "What's happening in your favorite TV soap operas," giving a weekly summary of adultery, murder, mayhem and all those things that people watch soap operas for.

Anyway, I've come up with this little scheme to torment the pathetic mopes whose lives revolve around the soaps, and you can help. Clip out this column, but be sure to cut across the bottom line below. Send the bottom half to an avid soap watcher. She will read it and think there are a number of soaps that she's been missing. It will drive her to distraction. If she doesn't have cable, she'll have it installed. If she does have cable, she'll probably buy one of those dopey satellite dish antennas so she can receive a couple of hundred more channels. Better yet, she might have a mental breakdown and wind up in a ward with a large male nurse who smokes non-filter cigarettes, has tattooed forearms and a Pete Rose haircut. What ever the results, it's worth a try.

- - - - - - - - - - - - -(cut along dotted line) - - - - - - - - - - - - -

WHAT HAPPENED IN THE SOAPS LAST WEEK

by Cuthbert Sims-Twit

"All Your Kids"—Eddie punches Mary in the mouth for telling her mother that he once sold waterless cookware. At the last minute John refuses sex with Sally but then explodes a

Cheddarwurst in the microwave. After breast reduction surgery, Rachel leaves Tom and returns to body-and-fender repair school.

"Another Place"—After the wedding, Howard tells Charlotte that he's gay, but only on weekends. Laura and John have a fight over entrées in a tapas bar. William loses his accounting practice when he admits he's dyslexic. Jason discovers that Jane buys her clothes at Lane Bryant.

"Central Hospital"—After falling from his bedroom trapeze bar, Dr. Kaufman begins speaking Esperanto. Madge confides to Beverly that she's turned on by men who wear welding goggles. Mona is diagnosed as schizophrenic when she tells Dr. Hastings she's on a first-name basis with Montovani. Bill becomes fascinated with Lava Lites.

"Santa Anna"—Tony and other ranch hands begin spending a lot of time together. Albert tells Gwen that he never wears underwear. Simon chokes to death on tapioca. Ralph reveals Kay's secret about the cattle prod. Bill Bob begins wearing chaps to bed.

"The Young and the Selfless"—Diane is killed by a falling lug nut. Jimmy buys a crossbow and shoots himself in the eye. Sandra tells Dave that she is not the mother of their children. Gary asks Raymond to choose between him and his personal computer. Josh's American Express card is cancelled. "

"As the World Churns"—Joe is blown to smithereens when the letter bomb he sends to Sean is returned postage-due. On her deathbed Aunt Elvira admits that she can't stand Frank Capra movies. Lonnie falls out of a tree and think's he's Joyce Kilmer. Gunther kicks the head off a pigeon.

Mamet in regular or relaxed, teal or taupe

THE FEBRUARY LANDS' END catalog arrived last week. Among the full-page spreads of beach scenes featuring cotton chinos and "Denim Done Right!" is a short essay on the art of writing and hanging out by Pulitzer Prize-winning playwright David Mamet. The accompanying sepia-toned photo shows a young writer seated at a lunch counter smoking a Lucky Strike and recording his thoughts with a $150 fountain pen. It might even be Mamet himself for all I know, but the person pictured looks as if he suits up at the Armani Exchange and would never split infinitives in "Rugged Rugby Knits that won't shrink out of fit" or "Men's Square Rigger Jeans" in either traditional or relaxed versions.

I read Mamet's piece, even the sentence, "Writing, in my experience, consists of long periods of hanging out, punctuated by the fugue of remorse at the loss of one's powers, and wonder at occasional output in spite of that loss."

I'd like to kick him hard in the spleen for that sentence. "Here's your fugue of remorse, Bozo," I'd say. "And didn't you rely on the F-word just a little too much in Glengarry Glen Ross? And that plot—c'mon."

But the truth is that he is a Pulitzer award-winning playwright and can punctuate fugues, sonatas and rondos of remorse anytime and any place.

Even more disturbing, he's loaded and probably has enough money for two lifetimes. He doesn't need a piece published in a Lands' End catalog.

But I do. I have a kid in college who is studying philosophy and another at home who wants to be a musician. I'll be financing my own senior daycare. Besides, I could use a little walking around money so I could hang out and drink coffee with great writers in the hopes that something would rub off (of them, not me).

And anyway, my home now contains enough Lands' End stock to qualify as one of their outlets. Not a month goes by without us ordering a kid's ski jacket or broadcloth shirts or a dozen other geegaws from that magic 800 number. They owe me a shot at the big time.

But here's the best part. It's not something I'm proud of, but I've written a good share of advertising. Read Mamet's essay and nowhere will you find any selling copy for Lands' End. But with writing like "That frantic and forced consumerism of the sports bar will not do; neither what has become the muddled and tense obsequiousness of that proclaiming itself The Restaurant," there's no room for selling copy. Why waste a couple of catalog pages if you're not going to hawk something?

That's why I've written a little piece on writing and hanging out in diners. Lands' End can include it in their March mailing.

I took a long, slow drag on my Camel as our eyes met across the crowded lunch counter. She was another one of those English lit hopefuls who think they can knock out a literary masterwork and complete a PhD the same semester. Maybe she could. She was organized enough with her Lands' End Deluxe Attaché. As the catalog says, it's "handsome enough for the boardroom, gutsy enough for the street." And speaking of gutsy, she was reading Anais Nin right there in the open. But then that's to be expected of a woman who wears a Denim Jumper—"even the name suggests ease"—over Pure Cotton Elastic Waist Weekenders. We were so young and casual then, as if life had no focus. A big trucker named Leo tried to lay his paws on her, so I shot him. I'm still doing time. The guys in C Block gave me a carton of cigarettes for wearing a pair of Ultra Blue Capri Pants—"you get our second skin fit that won't bind or tug."

Afterwards they punctuated my fugue.

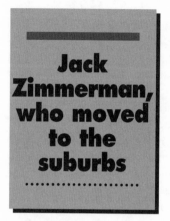

Jack Zimmerman, who moved to the suburbs

························

At the age of thirty Jack Zimmerman moved from Chicago to the suburbs determined to live the gamut of the suburban experience. He became a chauffeur for mouthbreathers, maintained a refrigerator full of microwavable chicken patties, taught Sunday school, and joined the Lions Club. He practiced lawn care and aluminum siding restoration. At last he knows the difference between soffit and fascia.

For ten years he has chronicled this life, two columns a week, in the Elmhurst Press. His writing has garnered two first place awards from the Illinois Press Association and free beers from local bartenders.

He wasn't always as you see him now. In a Lithuanian neighborhood on Chicago's South Side, he spent his early years listening to Charlie Parker, reading *Down Beat,* and playing trombone in his parents' basement. He heard a symphony orchestra for the first time when the Chicago Symphony came to his college in Quincy, Illinois. When the trumpet of Adolph Herseth floated above the orchestra, Zimmerman said, "Please, God, I've got to do this for a living."

He's been broke ever since.